MW00906870

Across this Silent Canvas

Hubbard Miller

Edited & Preface by William L. Spencer

First Edition

2005

Published by
Very Readable Books
P.O. Box 145, Pauma Valley, CA 92061
www.VeryReadable.com

Library of Congress Control Number: 2005937634

ISBN-10: 0-9776263-0-X
ISBN-13: 978-0-9776263-0-4

Printed in Canada

First Edition

9 8 7 6 5 4 3 2 1

For those whose turn comes next
to mark a place on the trail and
to signify how it was for us

Remembering Hub
a preface
by William L. Spencer

I wish this could be only about Hub, but I can only make it be about me at those times that Hub was there. I can't vouch for the perfect accuracy of all the details, and (assuming you're not reading this as part of your dissertation prep) that's not what you really want to know, anyway. So I will set this down partly the way it was for me at the time, and partly the way I know now that it probably was, and you can have it for what it's worth.

I tumbled off the back of the turnip truck at the University of Washington the autumn of 1954, driving from Coeur d'Alene, Idaho to Seattle with a high school classmate who had a car.

I had thought that Reed College in Portland, even in those long-ago days a hotbed of the liberal arts, was where I should go, but Reed required an essay as part of its application. The summer I was eighteen beside Lake Coeur d'Alene life was just too sweet and easy to bother with an essay. So I was off to the UW, where a high school transcript C+ average, a check for tuition and a pulse rate were all one needed.

I had made what today I remember fondly as my first adult decision when I chose not to go to the University of Idaho with the high-jinks-loving high school gang — I had a deep foreboding that would be fatal. I felt the need to strike out in another direction. I didn't know much, but I knew there was an awful lot I didn't know.

Back in those days I was a jazz drummer. My idol was the impeccable Max Roach, and I had a whole outfit for serious evening wear modeled on the most stylish Mr. B — Billy Eckstine, the legendary jazz vocalist.

I signed up for the University marching band. The first day of band practice, I was surprised to find I was the only student there who wasn't majoring in music. When this came to light, the band director gave me a sour look and a brief audition and then grudgingly let me stay. So there I was, the would-be jazz drummer from, of all places, Idaho, shown even during his first days at college to be a notable misfit.

I met Hub toward the end of that first week.

Reading Hub's piece *Blackberry* today, I can understand what he saw in me, since just two years before he had been the mis-placed cowpoke from Eastern Oregon.

Hanging out with Hub was a world of unexpected experiences.

We would be walking down the hallway of the music building in the evening, and Jo, an intense piano major, would pull Hub into one of the practice rooms to help her with something she was working on. Gordy would ask Hub to come over and listen to a Chopin etude and help him with phrasing. One Saturday Hub told me we were going to Marlene's. I had heard the name, Marlene was a piano major who could really *play*, but that's all I knew.

We drove across Seattle to a house on Mercer Island with floor to ceiling windows overlooking Lake Washington. I waited on a damask silk sofa while Marlene played on a grand piano with the top up and Hub paced, smoking and listening. What the hell is this all about, I wondered, who is this guy?

Everyone wanted a piece of Hub's musical ear, his insight and his understanding. They listened to him as though he were one of the professors.

Hub dragged me along on many of these occasions, maybe for company, maybe for my further edification, or perhaps to keep the situation from veering too much from the musical to the personal. Because it was more than the music. I can still see him in his characteristic pose, elbow cupped in one hand, holding a cigarette beside his face, a light shadowing of beard along his jawline, that little half-smile he had and the look in his eyes straight at you while he listened, taking in everything. Then he would reply and as often as not he addressed on the one hand what you had said, and at the same time the subtext of your entire personality and your fundamental assumptions about life. Too often it seemed as though Hub understood more about you than you knew about yourself.

With music, with literature, with social institutions, with people, with everything Hub played a game new to me: how perceptive can you be, how intuitive can you be?

For all that, when it came to jazz Hub was as square as they come. Here was a guy who called himself a composition major and he had never even heard of Thelonious Sphere Monk, much less the dress code of a hip dude at the clubs along Manhattan's 52nd Street. I called him Hube the Cube, or (once I had found out about Braque and Picasso) Hubist the Cubist, which was, I thought, the most appropriate monicker.

One weekend Hub took me home with him to Portland, where his family had moved from the ranch so his mother could receive the medical care she needed. For me Hub's family was like something out of a novel. His father, Earle, I was to learn during this and subsequent visits, liked nothing better than to sit down with the college boys and talk ideas. I always thought he would have been happiest as a professor of philosophy. Hub's mother, Marion, was quite ill with cancer. I was ushered into the room where she was propped up in bed, obviously weak, for a brief introduction.

Hub's brother, Jolly, short for Jolyon, was named after one of the characters in John Galsworthy's series of novels, *The Forsyte Saga*. Jolly was a handsome, charming star athlete at his high school. Hub's youngest brother, Lee, was the joker-clown of the family. But it was the open and loving warmth and pleasure that each family member so obviously felt for the others that was new to my experience.

And then, the next school year, Hub was gone.

"Where's Hub been? I haven't seen him lately."

"Didn't you know? He joined the Air Force."

"He what?"

"Quit school and joined the Air Force."

Those were the days of Universal Military Training and the Draft, for which we would all eventually become eligible. But Hub's move was unexpected and unexplained. One day he was just gone.

Hub was gone, but my education continued. Eventually, one early spring afternoon on the grass in front of Vernon Parrington Hall, I discovered the drama majors, a world in which I found an appealing combination of artistic activity, old fashioned pragmatism and certainly the prettiest girls on campus.

I came home to my father's house in Spokane at the end of my sophomore year to find that Hub had moved into the top bunk in my room and had created for himself the role of fair-haired boy in what passed at the time for my family. The dogs, Wimpy and Susie, loved him, and my step-mother Maxine and my father, a physician and surgeon, liked him a lot more than they had ever liked me.

Hub had insinuated himself completely into my family with no introduction on my part, all on his own. In addition to the surprise of finding him there, becoming the favorite son had the added bonus of being a little joke on me, as if to say, Jeez, Bill, your family is so easy to charm and manipulate, why haven't you bothered to do it?

Hub was an enlisted man in the Air Force, stationed at Fairchild Air Force Base just outside Spokane. My father called him Airman Miller.

The Air Force trained Hub as an electronic countermeasures technician. As the ECM tech, Hub flew from time to time on missions in the B-36, mainstay of the Strategic Air Command. At that time the U.S. was flying secret missions probing the radar capability and weaknesses of Cold War threat Russia. The ECM operator was responsible for the early detection of the Russian radar signals so that the plane could fly out at the edge of their range, where the plane could read their radar signals, but they couldn't detect the plane. In the event a missile was fired at the plane, the ECM operator had various counter responses available. Hub told me about flip-flops and gates, the technology of the earliest computers.

It was an immersion in electronics in the Air Force, and science around the house. The coffee table always held the latest issue of *Scientific American*, that month's edition of the *Journal of the American Medical Association*, and the odd copy of *American Rifleman* and *Field and Stream*. The glass-fronted bookcase in my room, which was more the extra room where things were stored, held back issues of the annals of the American Radio Relay League, Boccaccio's *Decameron* that contained some pretty hot stuff and Kraft-Ebbing's *Psychopathia Sexualis*, a study of sexual perversity, remembered, when it's remembered at all, for his coinage of the term sadism. We might not have been much for displays of affection around my father's place, but by God we were pretty damn well-read.

One summer we drove from Spokane to the Double Key Ranch, five thousand acres in Eastern Oregon. We travelled along part of the route Hub describes in *Journey Home*. Hub said he needed to visit his horse, Tabasco.

Those were the days before CDs, before eight-track tapes, even before FM. For music we had only the little AM band radio and the skunky sound of a distorting speaker in the dashboard of an aging Chevrolet. But it didn't much matter, because the only stations available were broadcasting either the top forty pop tunes or (more commonly) country-western music.

For me the long, tedious parts of the trip, as the endless hills of sagebrush rolled past, were made even more annoying because Hub had no sympathy for my malaise. He told me how on some car trips when he was alone he would imagine Mozart, Beethoven or some other figure from the past in the passenger seat and his task was to explain to them everything that had happened since they died, starting with their questions about the car itself, the speed, the highway, the billboards and of course the country-western music coming from the radio. I remember he said that Beethoven was a particularly bothersome guest — because he was deaf, Hub had to shout whatever he said to him.

Hub had an unusual capacity to entertain himself. Sitting on the beach at Lake Pend Oreille, in Northern Idaho where my father kept his boat, I would be in the doldrums, waiting impatiently for whatever was going to happen next, which I knew well enough was not very much, while Hub busied himself with the smooth glacier-and-river-rounded rocks. After a while I would look over and see that Hub had figured out how to stack this improbable material into a beautiful little model building that had kind of a Frank Lloyd Wright look to it. It's not just that he was able to enjoy himself and make something, but that he had made something *beautiful.*

Hub told me — maybe it was during the trip to the Double Key — that he was never bored, that everything was interesting, and that he didn't understand how anyone could be bored. He said that one time he had decided to try and experience complete and total boredom, so he planned an entire day, from morning to evening, doing absolutely nothing other than sitting in front of a television set watching daytime TV. It was the 50s. He figured, and I fully concurred as he told me this story, that this would be the most incredibly boring thing a person could possibly do. He said he started to watch the daytime soap operas and there wasn't much interesting in the content, but he began to pay attention to how one scene was designed to foreshadow and flow into the next, what the decision process must have been underlying a show or a dramatic construction. You can watch a soap opera, Hub maintained, and like a sort of cultural Rosetta Stone, extrapolate what the producers and writers assumed about their audience, and so gain an insight into their cultural assumptions, and therefore everyone else's cultural assumptions.

So as it turned out he wasn't bored at all by daytime television, but rather he found it somewhat intriguing.

Hub told me this story and I nodded and filed it away, wondering to myself at the time whether he had actually done that experiment, or whether he had just made it up in order to provide me with a little lesson in how to entertain myself. If he made it up as a clever instruction for Bill, then Hub's mind worked one way, but if he had actually undertaken that experiment, then his mind worked in another, perhaps more profound and disciplined way. Who in the world actually had enough patience and abstract intellectual curiosity to sit down and watch television all day (assuming, of course, they weren't some nitwit who actually *liked* daytime television)?

One of those summers after I had taken a creative writing class (the professor's wife had once dated Lennie Tristano, a blind pianist who played with Dizzy Gillespie and Charlie Parker during the bebop era), I was working on, I think, a play I called *No Deposit, No Return*. The title was taken from the notification that at the time appeared on soft drink and beer containers, as the bottling industry began its long and losing battle against the impetus for recycling. I'd been reading Jean-Paul Sartre, Albert Camus and Andre Gide, and I thought it was a pretty cool title. I was sitting around the living room in the evening scribbling on a yellow lined tablet.

Within a day or so Hub brought out his own yellow lined tablet and announced that he, too, was writing a play. His was called *Into the Weathers of Space Go I Unrehearsed.*

I was chagrined; his title was so much more emotionally evocative and pregnant with possibilities than was mine. Mine was the dead-end, his was everything in the future. Hub further needled me by never allowing me to read any of what he was writing, while he got to read and criticize all my stuff.

When I started putting this volume together, I at first thought that I would call it *Into the Weathers of Space Go I Unrehearsed.* But then I realized that however much I liked it, however affectionately I remembered it, it didn't fit. For one thing, by the time he got around to writing the pieces in this book, Hub knew well what the weathers of space portended, and he had had plenty of rehearsal. The tolling beauty of that phrase was, I think now, a recapitulation of his place in the world at that particular time: leaving the University, joining the Air Force, uncertain what would come next and unsure where he would land, like the wind-borne seeds of the thistle he describes in *Blackberry*.

In the spring of 1958 I graduated from the University. Not much was made of the event. My mother flew down from Alaska, where she was a nurse with the U.S. Public Health Service, and Hub drove over from Spokane. We went to dinner at a Chinese restaurant. That fall I was drafted into the Army. When I was discharged in 1960, I requested release at Fort Dix, New Jersey and caught the bus to New York, where Hub had moved with Jolly's help about six months before.

Hub and Jolly had been living in Seattle, where they had an old Chevrolet. They had sold it for (I think the figure was) five hundred dollars to a couple of acquaintances who did not have the money at the time, but promised to pay in the future. A year or so went by with no payments made for the car. In the meantime Hub decided to move to New York. So they called up the guys with the car, said they were moving, and could they borrow it. Since the guys had yet to make any payment for the car, they could hardly refuse. Hub and Jolly picked up the car, loaded their stuff into it and drove it to New York. It was still there, sitting on West 87th Street, when I arrived.

Those months in New York were post-graduate education in mid-20th century culture. Hub's aunt, Gladys Miller, Earle's sister, had moved to New York after college, and she was now one of the senior people at Holt, Rinehart and Winston, a publishing company on Madison Avenue. She was editor of two magazines for the company, had been the interior designer who redecorated Blair House, the government guest house across the street from the White House, and she was the author of a well-received book, *Decoratively Speaking*. She lived in a beautiful apartment at One University Place on the edge of Greenwich Village.

Gladys received complimentary tickets to performances at Carnegie Hall and the Metropolitan Opera, and she gave all her tickets to Hub. We went to every event at Carnegie Hall, where Leonard Bernstein conducted the New York Philharmonic.

These were also the golden years of live drama on television and New York was its center. Every week we went to Gladys' apartment to watch *The Play of the Week* and *Playhouse 90* on her television set, and it was there we saw Samuel Beckett's *Waiting for Godot* with Burgess Meredith and Zero Mostel. Ingmar Bergman's movies were reaching the U.S., and *The Seventh Seal* and *Wild Strawberries* were playing on a double bill at a theatre in Greenwich Village.

We saw everything, and everything was there in New York to be seen, even Leni Riefenstahl's classic propaganda ode to Hitler and the Nazi Party, *Triumph of the Will*, the whole uncut thing. Some afternoons I would wander across Central Park to the Metropolitan Museum of art, walk upstairs to the gallery on the south side of the building, sit down and look at El Greco's *View of Toledo*, just that one painting, nothing else. After a while I would walk home. The music, the movies, the television programs, the bars, the restaurants, the museums, the people — it was all grist for the mill.

Hub rented a second-floor-front apartment at 24 West 87th Street, just a half block from Central Park, and had enchanted Lena Staub, the little rotund landlady with a Middle European accent. "Helloo Meester Mee-lar," she would chime when she passed Hub on the stairs, and always want to stop and chat.

In *Little Brother* Hub writes, "Even at five years of age I could identify the emotional tenor of the performer from the sound of the instrument." I don't think that's an exaggeration. I know he could hear things before others heard them. He had a parlor trick I would cajole him into performing. As we walked down a New York street, Hub could hold up his arms, like Leonard Bernstein conducting Bartok's *Concerto for Orchestra,* and conduct the sounds of New York — the car and taxi horns, the sirens, the crash of the garbage trucks, all the sounds of that notoriously noisy city. He would give the little upward ready move, then the cue and the taxi bleat would be there, echoing through the

Manhattan canyons. For me and for others, we could at best wave a hand only just fractionally after the sound arrived. But somehow Hub could hear what was coming before it quite got there, or perhaps he was listening to the silences between sounds or picking up the city's tempo. I didn't know how he did it, and I could never figure it out.

The following year, the Army reserves on my heels, I left New York. Jolly and I drove the old Chevrolet back across the country pretty much non-stop. That trip was a novelette in itself.

I wish I had kept a journal of those years and written everything down in careful Boswellian fashion. But to do that I would have had to have been someone else, and then perhaps those things we thought and said and did and played at might have been entirely different. Maybe not even worth writing down at all. So there you have it, just like Hub's opening paragraph in *Measles*, a paragraph that rings so truly with his voice, "The insidiously irritating irony of it all is that . . . no matter how much one knows, one never knows for sure."

That's enough. The rest is Hub's book. I hope you enjoy it.

THE DOUBLE KEY

And yet, though I have been away, the concerts I play, the music I write, the ideas I pursue and the feelings I trust are but Eastern Oregon turned into music.

Once Upon a Time . . .

Though I treasure the vision that science has given me of man's true place in the universe, trapped inexorably between quark and quasar, it has done little to teach me how to live happily, except perhaps to underscore the fact that, if we are to survive at all, it will be by our own doing and not by some miracle from above.

Knowledge has brought me to see how each tiny element relates to every other, how the processes of coming to be is one vast story with no part out of place.

And yet for all the power of this understanding, power to change the very face of the earth, power to place one species dangerously above all others, all this power has not added one whit to wisdom. For wherever one looks, whether at the sub-nuclear game of quantum chance, or the mirrored halls of the castle of consciousness or the unreachable whirlings of galactic light, at the edges our power fades into the unknowable.

There we find ourselves once again sitting on a log, staring out across a beautiful sea at a sunset, and wondering at it all. And what can we say that improves one comma upon the Buddha, or Sophocles, or Shakespeare or Thoreau, or any man of great spirit?

There on the beach our children play, building sand castles, skipping rocks, asking questions. What do we say? I know that I wish them to understand at least those things which I have come to value. And as I search through my own mind asking, "How did I come to learn these things?" I am led back to the people and ways and lessons and experiences that shaped me. For it was these values that formed a skeleton around which I might grow, that sustained me during hard times and confusion, and upon which I could hang knowledge when it came along.

So it is that during the day I talk about the tides and show the children fossils and answer why this and why that. And at night I try to explain the phases of the moon and show them how to find the North Star from the Big Dipper. Later, after they have been dried out and fed and tucked into their sleeping bags, I settle down with them for a while, and the murmuring ocean and the crackling fire draw me back to the time when I was them, and I hear my father saying, "Once upon a time . . ."

The Fighting Chickens, Treasure Island, and The Veecees

Once upon a time in a world that seems much different than the one you know, but was really much the same, there lived a little boy who was very lucky.

If you could see him and talk to him, you might not think he was lucky at all. He had no roller skates, no basketball, not even a bicycle. That was because where he lived there was nothing smooth and flat enough for rolling skates, riding bicycles, or bouncing balls; no sidewalks, no streets, no playgrounds. Besides, even if there had been a tennis court, who would he have played with? It was many miles from where he lived to the nearest house, and that house had no children his age.

His school had only one room, one teacher and six students, none of them in his grade. His little brothers were too young for anything but gurgling or crying in their diapers. His father and the men were busy working. And his grandmother, although she was fun to talk to, was not very good at games.

He got to see a movie only once a year when they went on vacation to the big city, and although they were not poor, his family had only one old wooden radio that barely worked once in a while. They had no records or record player, and television had not been invented yet. There were no comics to look at for no newspaper was delivered to their door. There were no Cub Scouts, no music lessons, no Little League, not even Sunday School or candy stores. And none of his T-shirts said Rolling Stones or Star Wars — they were all plain white.

Perhaps because all these forms of entertainment were missing, one activity that consumed much time and energy in those days was teasing and practical jokes. Whether it was just the ranchers in Eastern Oregon, or whether it was everyone at that time, teasing and practical jokes were developed into an art form. If you bragged too much about some skill or achievement, or if you let it be known that you thought you, or your horse, or your dog was superior in any way, you had better watch out.

When, for example, Uncle Jack got a new car of which he was very proud, a car that looked greatly out of place when parked next to the beat up, rusty ranch vehicles aged by weather and rough roads, it was too much to resist. After Sunday dinner it was only natural for someone to "borrow" it on some pretext, then go out and rev up the motor while a hidden partner crashed garbage can lids together, and a pre-set messenger delivered, "Oh, my God,

Jack's new car!" Everyone was there to watch Jack rush from the house cursing. But the boy's favorite practical joke, one that his father dreamed up, involved fighting chickens.

Cock fighting is one of the gruesome things that men do. Although it is legal only in three states (Oregon is not one of them), there is a strong tradition behind it and chickens are bred and trained, bought and sold, matched and fought and heavily bet upon.

Many a Sunday afternoon back in those days, you could find the cowboys and ranchers gathered around the corrals of Eastern Oregon cheering on, and betting upon, their favorites as the local cocks were matched and fought to the death. As man is wont to do, they improved upon nature by attaching to the roosters' natural spurs long steel blades that drew blood, shortened the fight, and insured death as the price of defeat.

Now it so happened that their neighbor rancher over the hill behind the house, Cliff Hillman, was very much into fighting chickens. He was a nice enough fellow, and the boy saw him often when he rode through the Hillman's pasture on his way to school. Cliff had just purchased a fine fighting cock from California, of which he was very proud. To hear him tell it, he was going to clean up. But he must have bragged just a little too much, for the boy's father, who did not approve of chicken fights, felt it was time to take Cliff down a notch.

"Ah, hell, Cliff," he said, when shown the new champion for the third time, "my barnyard rooster could whip that thing any day."

What Cliff didn't know was that the barnyard rooster was actually a fighting cock for which the boy's father had paid one hundred dollars in La Grande, with the express purpose of beating Cliff's favorite.

Meanwhile, back at the ranch, La Grande, as we called the new cock, had been turned loose in the barnyard and was surveying his new domain.

"Mighty fine," he crowed. "There are even a few scrawny hens around to begin my flock." For La Grande was not alone, chickenwise. Living there also was a flock of bantam chickens who made the ranch their home. We had not bought them, we never fed them, and we did not harvest them or their tiny eggs. They were just there, most probably the remnants of some fighting stock from fifty years earlier. They were hardy little things that asked for nothing, but announced the morning grandly, and were quick to give warning should a rattlesnake appear.

Guiding this flock on its daily routine were two small red and black banty roosters, who managed to share peaceably the hens between them, and by the time Cliff came over the hill to examine his challenger, Nip and Tuck, for so we called the bantams, had spotted La Grande. They were not pleased. Here was a great white monster rooster on their turf, and he was already eyeing their hens. Deep within their brainstems, juices flowed and war was declared.

A chicken fight is much like a dance, a barnyard ballet. They begin by marking off a circle with their strutting, about twenty-five feet apart, seemingly oblivious to one another. If either contender were to widen this distance, it would probably be considered a surrender, and the matter would end. But if neither chicken backs off, the circle gradually shrinks, slowly, slowly, each cock staying on the opposite side of the circle from his challenger, until the distance has closed to about three feet. At that point, as if responding to the referee's bell, suddenly they face each other, and with much sarcastic clucking, crowing and wing flapping, the fight begins. Their principal weapons for fighting are the spurs on the heel of each foot, and their technique is to jump atop their enemy, grab hold with their beak to stay aboard, and dig viciously with the spurs into the opponent's back. The fighter on bottom is in trouble, but he has the advantage of a free beak, with which he can peck at the eyes of the chicken on top. When this happens, the upper chicken must release his hold to save his sight, and falls off, and then the chickens square off for another go at each other.

Partly because La Grande was accustomed to fighting cocks his own size, and partly because he was counting on artificial spurs, which he did not have, that is not the way this fight went at all. When he jumped, he jumped too high. Nip, the first banty to challenge him, scurried underneath, kicking La Grande from behind, and receiving no blow at all. La Grande was perplexed, but tried again. Same result. If only once he could get hold of the smaller banty, it would all be over. His heavy legs, even without spurs, would club the banty senseless. But the banty was strong, quick and determined.

When we first noticed what was happening, it seemed only humane to stop the fight. After all, it wasn't fair to match the poor little banty with an experienced fighting cock twice his size. But as we watched, we began to realize to our amazement that little Nip was doing quite well. Still, it was a dangerous game, and at each pass Nip was tiring, getting a little slower. Again we considered stepping in. But then something happened that amazed everyone, and cast a whole new light on the affair. When they say that birds of a feather flock together, they aren't kidding. In what seemed to be a choreographed swap that happened so fast La Grande hardly noticed, Nip ran out and Tuck ran in. Bango, La Grande had a new fresh fighter to face, and the odds changed dramatically. Tuck continued the same successful strategy that had worked for Nip, and by the time they switched again, it was obvious that La Grande was in trouble.

After several more swaps, La Grande became so exhausted and confused that the little banty dared to jump atop him. The instant that happened, the other banty flew in to join in the *coup de grâce* and, had we not been there to separate them, it would have been the end of La Grande.

Of course, the practical joke was ruined. Early on, Cliff had figured out that the white rooster was a plant, intended to match his champion. But everyone, including the boy's father, was so taken with the afternoon's events, that the loss of the joke seemed small. In fact, it had gone just as planned, since the real barnyard rooster, in this case roosters, had defeated the fighting cock. Nip and Tuck were overnight heroes, proudly displayed to ranch visitors, and talked about at chicken fights and over chicken dinners throughout the county.

So you see, even without all the things boys and girls do today, life on the ranch was rich. There was hardly enough time in the day for eating, working, playing, learning and being surprised by the unexpected things that happened. Things like thunderstorms, falling stars, the birth of a calf or the death of a favorite old horse, the arrival of unexpected guests or the passing of the seasons. But a great part of everyone's life is spent sleeping. And because they got up at four or five in the morning, bedtime came early — eight o'clock in the winter when the nights were dark and frozen silent, perhaps as late as ten in the summer when it was barely dark enough for sleeping.

Every family has their own special going to bed rituals: having a snack, brushing your teeth, laying out out your clothes for tomorrow, gathering kisses, being tucked in, saying your prayers. But for the boy, the highlight of it all was the bedtime story. Not stories read from a book like his mother did. As good as those were, they were not so fine as stories told by heart, stories that were processed by the mind and imagination of the teller whom you knew and loved so well, stories with the lights out, the eyes closed, and the television of the mind running.

At night when all was ready, his father would come in, turn out the light, lie down on the bed, scratch himself, yawn, and begin: "Once upon a time . . ."

Many of these were stories from his father's own childhood, probably stretched a little or edited to make them less factual but more true. Stories about the dog, Flash, jokes he had played on his sisters (imagine having a sister!), tales of the old days when things were just as they seemed. Many of them, however, as the boy found out years later, turned out to be personalized adaptations of famous myths and fables; the journeys of Odysseus with his father in the title role; Earle slays the giant Goliath or visits the center of the earth, and watered down versions of *Huckleberry Finn*, *Moby Dick* and *Treasure Island.* Sometimes they were just improvised fantasies, taking off from some recent event the boy had shared, and moving willy-nilly through a mixture of fact and fiction, history and wish, half-remembered, half-created flotsam and jetsam that dwell in a man's mind.

Often they were more than stories. They were teachings and lessons, too, passing on, through the vehicle of romance, knowledge and rules that needed to be learned. Thus, when the Second World War began, the nightly story might be a travelogue of some imaginary pilgrim imparting meaning to the words Europe, England, France, Germany, Jews, Russians and war. Or again, when the father became aware that the boy and his friends had been experimenting with cigarettes in the barn, rather than confront the issue directly, he used a bedtime story. A terrible tale about the Tillamook Burn, a massive forest fire that had actually happened in Oregon. All of the destruction was dramatized — the forest gone, the wildlife fled and dead, the human loss and suffering. But in this tailored version, it all began with some careless boys smoking in a barn, boys who would in the future be much more careful, boys who could never again strike a match without lighting up in their own minds those powerful visions of animals fleeing and burned out snags silhouetted against a sky where smoke turned day to night for a thousand miles and the earth itself was changed forever.

Frequently the art of story-telling was combined with the art of teasing, as it often is in good adventures. A brilliant beginning, full of all the things boys love to hear, would be interrupted at the worst possible moment with endless diversions and details, putting off the resolution until it hurt. This technique leaves the hero dangling on a cliff while the storyteller lists the menu of the dinner he will eat if he should be so lucky as to escape. For example, the boy could never forget how he first heard *Treasure Island.* His father began the evening's session: "I had the most fantastic dream last night . . ."

And proceeded to tell a personalized version of the famous tale in which the father, the boy and his friends were the principal characters. A map was discovered (in the old barn), a journey was planned and undertaken to Cannon Beach (where his great-grandmother lived). There were many adventures along the way, including the teaming up with a fantastic Black man named Friday. The treasure was finally located under the sand behind Haystack Rock, exposed only at the lowest of tides, and brought up to the beach to be opened. But just at that moment, according to this version, the father awakened, and lying there in the darkened room, he excitedly said to his anxious listeners, "I've been waiting all day to ask you, *what was in that chest?*"

As the boy grew older and stronger, he found himself more and more often acting like an adult. In the morning his little brothers brought in the cows and he did the milking. During the day his little brothers drove the stacker team back and forth while he, atop the stack, wielded the pitchfork laden with feed for the winter. At Christmas the joy of giving gifts gradually overpowered the excitement of receiving them. And at bedtime, he found himself in the role of storyteller.

At first he tried repeating the tales his father had told many years ago. And while some of the better ones that he had heard many times seemed to work, many of them did not. The listeners could tell that he was not the real thing, that he was not old enough to have done or remembered the things he was talking about, that he was pretending to be something he was not. So more and more often, he found himself telling real tales from his own short life, admittedly exaggerated, but convincing in their setting. He had learned from his father how to take a simple adventure and flesh it out with description and detail, postponing the climax until it was time to go to sleep. He had learned how to make the characters in his stories the listeners themselves, and yet, by calling them different names or placing them in a far away setting, prevent them from objecting when the fiction touched closely on the facts. And he had learned how to combine teasing with tale telling.

Also he learned how to prepare himself in advance. How to watch throughout the day for events or settings that might make a good bedtime story. How to take something that someone had said at the breakfast table as a starting point, and then during the day, as he was driving the tractor and harrow round and round the field in what was an otherwise boring and repetitious chore, occupy his mind by assembling that night's tale.

Perhaps the best story he ever told, one that his little brothers remember still, began one day as he was leafing through a comic book reading the advertisements. Diamond rings for two dollars and fifty cents (or five for ten dollars), muscle building apparatus, books about the secrets of life as discovered in some Egyptian tomb, secret code rings, and things to amaze your friends. He found there an ad for glow-in-the-dark paint. For one dollar, plus postage, it offered a small bottle of phosphorescent fluid, and reflecting on the possibilities this presented, he invented the Veecees.

Since he had to wait two whole months for the bottle to arrive, he had a great deal of time to set this one up, to drop the invented word Veecees around pregnantly, to come upon and report strange happenings, to sight flying saucers (they were big then), to fashion in his listeners' minds a soft spot that he could later touch upon. Finally the bottle arrived, and after some secret experiments, he was ready to spring the trap.

In the early days everyone had their own bedroom, but as little brothers, cousins and friends multiplied, this became impractical. A garage at the back of the house had been converted into a sleeping porch where all of the children slept together in one great bed-filled room. It had no windows, but a garage door which could be opened when the weather was hot. Usually it was closed and the room dark, even during the day, for naps. It was in this setting that over the years all of the children, each snuggled into his own bed, had listened to the nightly tales. And it was this room that the boy prepared for the invasion of the Veecees, by secretly covering the walls and ceiling with invisible (with the lights on) dots and patterns of glow-in-the-dark paint. That night when Jolly and Lee, Stuart and John, Catlin and Susan and Ann bedded down for their nightly story, he made certain that one dim light remained on.

He told them then of the *Veecees*. Strange creatures from outer space who flew around in flying saucers (had they not heard of them? They had!). The Veecees were slowly taking over the earth. The army was powerless against them. Even the atomic bomb did not penetrate their defenses. They had already taken over several countries in South America, and the government had asked all citizens to report anything unusual. They were very fond of out of the way, remote places like Wallowa County. He reminded the children of the strange things that had been happening around the ranch lately, things he had carefully constructed and pointed out to them over the last month. And finally, after much description of the things they had done, of the planet they came from, and of their journey to earth, he pointed out the terrible fact that they were invisible. Invisible except for one thing . . . *They glowed in the dark!*

I will leave you to imagine what happened after this tale, when the boy finally said good night, got up and left the room, turning out the light on the way. I will tell you this much; it took about ten seconds before he heard Johnny say, "What's that?"

Much to his mother's dismay, it was hours before everyone was back in bed and asleep.

The boy and the little brothers and the cousins and friends are all grown up now, and most of them have children of their own. They almost all live in big cities and they all have bicycles, roller skates, television, video games, and much more. They all have teasing and practical jokes, and a few of the lucky ones have bedtime stories, too. But I know that their parents must wonder sometimes when they are put upon to buy new batteries, new tapes, trips to Disneyland or any of the millions of things which children today take for granted, if they would not perhaps be better off with a personal version of *Treasure Island* or the *Veecees*.

It is always easy to romanticize childhood, remembering the good times and forgetting the bad, and it is all too common for the old to question the ways of the young. But it is nice to know that one does not need the things of today to be rich and happy, that there are many ways to live and learn and love, and that the ways of here and now are but one of them.

Peanuts, Popcorn, Brownie, Bones, Horrible . . . and Jesus

When I had my eleventh Christmas the calendars all said 1945. But on the ranch where we lived in the Snake River country of Eastern Oregon, it might as well have been 1845. For the technology, the traditions and the tempo by which we lived were still wholly governed by natural cycles.

The day began at dawn and ended at dark and temperature was more important than taxes. The moon was our memo from management, measuring the progress of our planting, bewitching our beasts, lighting the way up the lane at night or keeping us in the dark. And the great slow swing of the seasons formed the longest cycle we could feel in our bones, next to life itself.

On a cattle ranch, you don't keep many milk cows. Just enough to provide you with dairy products. And at eleven, my hands were just big enough so that I had been given the very real responsibility of milking. It wasn't easy, and there were mornings when I hated it. But it did have it's rewards: the sweet smell of a flank in your face at five in the morning and the pride of providing an important resource.

But most of all the chance to develop a lasting relationship with some of creation's most profound creatures, cows.

Without the cow and horse, or the goat and camel in other climates, man would not be programming space missions today. Even now, if cows were to vanish, half the world would starve. And there was a point, not too long ago, when the cow and the horse were essential steps on our climb out of darkness.

To keep a family supplied in milk, you must keep more than one cow, because periodically they must freshen (have a calf) to keep the milk flowing. Even two cows is risky if you are dependent on their output, because keeping the cycles of freshen and dry-up, ovulation and gestation, coordinated is impossible. So we had several cows. From each of them I learned something important. And in some way each of them contributed to Christmas 1945.

Some time in September my father found me building a fort in the baled hay and asked me if I would mind riding down to the third bluegrass to put out a stray that he had noticed. This would be my introduction to Horrible. I was a little resistant because at the moment nothing was more important than my fantasy world of secret hiding places, but he insisted that it had to be done now. So I went out and brought in the horses, saddled up Tabasco, and headed down Prairie Creek through the valley bottom pastures that we called the bluegrasses, first, second and third. It was a beautiful fall day, and once away I was delighted at the prospect of something to do and the whole wide world to do it in. It was about two miles to where I was headed, and I passed the time marking magpie nests for future robbery and talking to Tabasco about lie detectors and dinosaurs, two of my current fascinations, one from Dick Tracy the other from *Fantasia*.

Halfway through the third bluegrass I saw Horrible standing alone at the foot of the pasture right in front of the gate that I had to put her through. This will be easy, I thought . . . except for her ears! She had noticed me already, and was alert with that kind of devilish anxiety that indicates disaster when driving cattle. She was an ugly cross breed, a “honyock” with a big floppy milkbag that swung grossly back and forth as she moved, and a tail that swiped her own output all over herself and anything else within range. Worse still, she was “on the prod,” which is Eastern Oregon for angry, frightened and nothing but trouble. Since I had to open the gate first anyway, I used cattle-moving technique number one: I ignored her. Tabasco and I ambled slowly on as if she didn’t exist, and I got off, opened the gate, and stopped by the creek to drink. But she was not to be tricked. By this time she was halfway across the pasture, pawing the earth, snorting her snotty nose, and pointing at us as if we were Frankenstein and an alien from outer space.

For the next hour-and-a-half Tabasco and I lathered ourselves up with every trick in the cowboy book on how to get a cow through a gate. But each time she neared the gate she would bolt and run on a frantic spree, as if she and the gate were repelling one another like the same poles of magnets. Across the creek, through the brush, scratch your legs and poke your eye, back across the creek into the fence, the staples scream and the barbed-wire sings, run, stop, turn, bluff, wait, all to no avail.

Gradually I began to realize that I wasn't going to be able to get her out, and with that came a feeling of failure and resentment. I knew that I had done a damn good job, that even Tommy, our top puncher, could not have licked Horrible alone. But I also knew that, when I got back to the ranch with the job undone, Dad would grab the horse, already exhausted, saying something like, "That's all right, I'll do it."

And that is just what happened when I arrived home crying with defeat. I even cursed, which at that age was severely frowned upon, and therefore highly effective. Except of course that, seeing the lather, Dad got a fresh horse. Embarrassed to be seen by the men in that state, I went to the house where Mother, in her wisdom, offered the following diversion: It was time to order Christmas presents.

Since we went to town maybe once a month, and that town, Joseph, was small and limited, most of our outside things came from mail order, in particular Montgomery-

Ward. But delivery was long and slow and Christmas had to be anticipated by several months. Furthermore, since Santa Claus had recently been elevated from a mere man to a spirit in my mind, and since I had a little money of my own from a 4-H Club calf, I was about to discover the great joy of giving gifts.

Christmas 1945 was special. The war was over and many things that had been rationed or unavailable were suddenly there for the asking. Furthermore, one could get into the frivolous and the romantic without the guilt of knowing that others were fighting and dying.

I spent the remainder of the afternoon in my room with the door closed pouring through the catalogue, adding and re-adding the numbers. The only difficulty was Mother's present, for she had to check the forms and figures without knowing which present was hers. Also, I had ordered one present for myself, which, because of its nature, rather stood out. In any case, Mother pretended not to notice what might be for her and what I had chosen for myself, and everything went beautifully.

When Dad arrived home after dark, late for dinner and in a state much as I had been, I received my first Christmas present early. For Horrible was still in the bluegrass. In fact, she had broken through into the second bluegrass then into the first. Had it been light we could have seen her across the valley, practically in front of the house. The next day it took Tommy, Dad and I to finally get poor

Horrible cast out, and even then it wasn't easy. But I remember old Tommy's comment as he finally closed the gate on her. "Poor critter," he said, spitting a wad of tobacco juice at the rock-jack that held up the gate. "Ain't no good gonna come to her."

Since that day I have met many a Horrible, creatures who, through accident of birth or upbringing, have come to misunderstand, then to fear and hate the world they live in. Because they are sick and hopeless, they are cast out of whatever pasture they invade. And while I have long since learned not to let them get my goat, to understand why they are the way they are, and to pity their condition, neither science nor art has improved upon Tommy's observation: "Poor critter."

I think of Popcorn rather the same way I think of Marilyn Monroe or Judy Holiday: a cute, dumb blonde with just a touch of pathos about her. She was a Guernsey, giving a fair amount of good milk, easy to handle, but lacking a certain maternal depth of character. I recall that even in middle age she would occasionally frisk around the frosty barnyard like a calf, or suddenly take it into her head to challenge the dogs. She was friendly and well-behaved, easy to milk, never stepping in the bucket or arguing about which stall to enter. But while I liked her a lot, I felt that our relationship would never deepen. During that fall Popcorn was the principal supplier of milk. Peanuts was dried up and pregnant, and Bones was, except in emergency, used to fatten calves and show stock, rather than for human consumption.

Then one snowy morning around pumpkin time, when Tippy brought the cows into the barn lot, I noticed that Popcorn was limping on her left hind foot. I checked her over for something stuck between the cloves of her hoof, or a nail, the usual things, but I could discover nothing. We had trimmed her hooves about a week before and I figured that maybe they were a bit short. But the next day she was worse, her milk supply was down, and the morning after that she did not appear at all. On request, Tippy led me to her, standing forlornly under a winter-bare willow, and what I saw was sad. Her whole hind leg was swollen below the knee to twice its normal size. Her eyes were glassy, and her spirit weak. Popcorn had what looked to be foot-rot, only much worse than usual. I suppose that nowadays it may be treatable, and we did the best we could with huge injections of sulfa into the jugular, keeping her in the barn with hay to eat and soaking the afflicted foot with various home remedies.

Reflecting back, I wonder if that is truly what she had, for most cases cured that way. But you can't keep a cow in intensive care forever, and we had long since learned that the barn was the most dangerous place for sick animals. With all due respect to medicine, more often than not the animals did best when left alone for nature to run its course.

But Popcorn wasn't just any cow. She was a family friend, and as a result we hung on to hope much longer than usual. Furthermore, I had become emotionally involved. Because I was milking I felt responsible for her welfare. As irrational as it may seem, Popcorn's troubles were laid at my door. And surely prayer and love would work.

For several nights I held her head in my lap and watched the light in those big, bulging, bovine eyes gently fade, and the comic-book-curled lashes close more and more often. I talked to her of spring, and I promised her a calf to keep for her very own. And I talked to her of God.

My family was what you would call loosely Protestant. Our catechism consisted of the Golden Rule, the Ten Commandments, the Lord's Prayer, the Twenty Third Psalm and above all else, the Truth, no matter how bad it hurt. But we rarely went to church, and although we said the blessing and were officially married and buried, for the most part it was between God and us. But at eleven one needs a little more structure than that, and I had just discovered religion, partly through music and partly through my Catholic friends. The Protestant burden of individual conscience was heavy to bear, and I longed for the rituals and reassurances a Catholic authority provided. Faced with a death in the family for the first time, I was having a crisis not only in terms of my responsibilities as shepherd of the milk cows, but in my most basic philosophy.

My father, bless his heart, knowing that Popcorn was a goner, and recognizing the seriousness of my feelings, gave me a gift which I have treasured all my life. Explaining to me that, since she must die anyway, letting her suffer was inhumane, he included me in the manly responsibility of being present when a bullet was placed in her brain, sending her off to greener pastures forever. Nothing could have saved me from the sorrow of that circumstance, but in following it through to the bitter end, watching and understanding, I learned that a man's ultimate responsibility to those he loves is to see that they die with mercy and dignity.

Then, once again, Christmas intervened to elevate what had happened into an even more meaningful event. For the very day we hitched up the team, Pride and Joy, and dragged poor Popcorn down the valley to the boneyard — a small triangular patch of trees where we took carcasses to keep the coyotes away from the buildings — that very day, like the twisted intricacies of an Italian opera plot, the package of Christmas presents arrived from Monkey-Wards.

No possible event could have been more timely. First, because it was great therapy to scuttle the box into my bedroom and explore each prospective present thoroughly, comparing it with my expectations and delighting in how well I had chosen. They were perfect. They were more than perfect. How could I ever wait until Christmas? But you may recall that I had ordered one gift for myself, and perhaps now you will understand why the arrival of that box on that exact day meant so much to me. It was a crucifix, very much like those I envied, and it was to go in my room as testament to my devotion.

Now, however, I had a new and far more important use for it. Once again Tabasco and I trailed down the valley to the boneyard. And there, on the stump of a willow, we placed the cross, sanctifying this graveyard with all the ceremony we could muster, and making peace with Popcorn and the forces of destiny.

Life went on, the days shortened and winter set in as the earth moved toward perihelion where the year ends and begins. With Popcorn gone and Peanuts not yet freshened, Bones was up. If there was a clown in this collection she was it: a big, black and white Holstein who, as her name suggested, had a canvassy hide stretched awkwardly over an unbelievable frame. Imagine a bovine basketball player who had been through a famine, or an ambulating oil derrick wrapped as a present. Her skinniness was not due to lack of food, however; she ate half-again as much as the other cows, but she never gained an ounce. It all went into milk. What Bones lacked in quality she made up for in quantity. Her bag was enormous with eight teats, six of which worked, and twice a day she gave many gallons of weak, watery milk, usable for cooking or cottage cheese, but nearly undrinkable.

Normally Bones suckled calves, providing supplementary calories to fatten registered show cattle. I don't know whether you can picture the absurdity of watching a two-year-old Hereford bull nursing, but such are the vagaries of the cattle business. Then there were times when Bones played surrogate mother, providing life to a calf whose mother had died, sometimes several calves at once.

So Bones was not accustomed to having human hands tap her resources, and milking her was an ordeal. I had to hobble her hind legs to keep her from stepping in the bucket, and tie her tail down to keep it from flailing my face. Even more distracting was her propensity to suddenly arch her back and pee, with little or no warning. Many times I had to throw out a bucket of milk and start over.

In spite of this, the more I got to know Bones the better I liked her. For one thing, she was glad to see me. You didn't have to send the dog out for her; she was waiting at the gate at milking time, because the pressure of milk in her bag was so great I am sure it was painful and milking a relief. Also, winter having covered the pastures with ice and snow, the shocks of hay I threw out twice a day and the ration of oats in the stanchion were food. And food to a hypoglycemic like Bones was where it was at. In fact, she would follow me around the barn lots and pastures as I did the chores, a bucket of grain here, chopping water holes in the ice there, shoveling out a space in the snow for the gate to swing, or adding to the steaming pile of manure that grew each winter, like a volcano, outside the barn.

Our conversations were friendly but not very profound. I told her about being eleven, she told me about being a cow. Her philosophy was simple: Use me if you must, but feed me. And in spite of her awkward, clumsy, crashing-into-things utilitarian body, she was happy, and she was beautiful. I think probably it was because, unlike the other milkcows, she got to nurse calves, thus fulfilling her maternal needs. I asked her about it but the only answer I got was the swipe of a fly with her tail and a longing look at the grain bin. That is to say, "Do your duty and don't worry about it." And I have to admit that, uninspiring as it is, this recipe has definite survival value.

By turkeytime the lack of drinkable milk at the table was getting to be too much, and my mother, though she was a delicate and beautiful woman, put her foot down: my children must have milk. So it was that Brownie arrived, a Brown Swiss the exact opposite of Bones. She was graceful and petite, with four tiny teats that gave, at best, one gallon a day. But it was good milk to drink and after crossing the six-week desert of milklessness, it tasted of ambrosia. One couldn't get enough. And thus, as a lesson in how sometimes a little is worse than none at all, it introduced into that time of the year especially devoted to giving, an element of avarice. For if you try to divide a gallon, minus some for the cats and cooking, among eight mouths, finely tuned to this taste, you come up a little short. And children, especially siblings, are natural competitors.

It was our custom that the table was set with a glass of milk at each place (except for Mother who didn't care for milk), and that any remaining was placed in a pitcher on the table, available to whomever first requested it. It did not take us long to discover that the pitcher emptied long before the requests. Thus our blessing became, "For what we are about to receive, O Lord, we are truly thankful," all spoken as rapidly as decorum permitted, followed by glug, glug, glug, "Please pass the milk," followed by arguments about who finished first, and who got extra milk yesterday, and I'll trade you milk for doing the dishes, and all manner of combative divisiveness.

It was only briefly funny. We were talked to, we were sent to our rooms, we were spanked even, as Mother and Dad tried to cope with an impossible situation. When absolute rationing was instituted, the worst happened: milk thievery. Missing from the icebox. I don't know who did it, but I must admit that, since I did the milking I got a couple of squirts in the mouth that never reached the pail.

Christmas always has difficulties woven into its fabric: impossible expectations, irritating excitement, unwanted or demanding guests and relatives, plus the inevitable upset of the everyday routine, and I am sure that this undercurrent exaggerated the milk war. I know that I, with my precious gifts all wrapped and ready to go, was in a state of Christmas fever like never before. This year I would be Santa Claus and like a singer before a performance, I was high strung.

Christmas Eve came upon us with its maelstrom of traditions: visits to friends, visits from friends, singing, stories, and food beyond reason, with a hyper-intensity in each gesture almost like a drug experience. It is, after all, a deeply meaningful occasion — the rebirth of the sun echoing down from Stonehenge, Bethlehem, and our own childhood expectations. Ghosts of Handel, Dickens, Botticelli and Dylan Thomas reflecting off tinselly balls of Hallmark, Bing Crosby and Mickey Mouse. Cross-cultural carols mixing myths with all the care of a clothes dryer. Santa's sleigh is filled with virgin conceptions, stockings hung from five-pointed stars, turkey and trees, mangers and mistletoe. But all for the children, of course. And I was at the peak of it, able to participate as both child and adult, riding the crest of a wave of good feelings that had been travelling for thousands of years.

Then the wave crashed against the rocks of milklessness when Mother discovered that the wee portion she had set aside for eggnogs was missing. To this day I do not know why I was blamed for it, there must have been some incriminating evidence. But I was innocent, and with justice seemingly buried in a snowdrift, eleven years of fury fought back. Choosing the only weapon that I possessed, I brought my presents from their hiding place in my bedroom, hurled them at the tree with a vindictive "Merry Christmas!" and fled into the night, fully confident that I would never return.

Oh, what a night it was. Drifted snow sparkling in the moonlight, the mountain peaks standing as an awesome audience as the stars sang like angels in a heaven of deep, deep blue. Just as God Himself might celebrate the birthday of his son. Even through my tears and troubles, it spoke to me of years gone by, and years to come, and the glory of something beyond. I saddled up Tabasco and, without quite knowing where I was going, headed down the valley to Popcorn and the cross now buried deep beneath the snow.

How she got there I will never know. She should have been up near the barn and shelter. But a pregnant cow has an instinct that, when her time is near, she should leave the herd and go off by herself. For there, in the boneyard, standing at the very edge of the frozen creek, was Peanuts, deep in the labor of giving birth.

If Horrible was an outcast, Popcorn a dancing girl and Bones a clown, then Peanuts was a saint. A little tan Jersey, calm and motherly, old and wise, with just the stump of one crooked horn, and deep brown eyes that understood at a glance, and cared.

She gave a fair amount of rich milk that separated into thick golden cream fit to top a king's dessert, and sweet milk that I shall long for till we meet again. She was too busy for me and my troubles, busy about bringing into the world the future of cattledom, and in so doing acting out her reason for being.

Studying the trail of hoofprints, laying places, blood, tissue and fluid in the snow, I could see that she had been at it for a long time. There is an almost overwhelming desire to help out in this sacred ritual, but there is really nothing one can do. I had long since learned not to meddle, that though I could not bear the pain and the waiting, she could.

There, in the silence of the winter night, faced with the reality of Peanuts' agony and glory, my petty problems melted into puddles at my feet.

Within fifteen minutes I could determine that progress was being made. Two tiny white hooves, front feet, were pointing out at the universe. In ten minutes more the whole forelegs and tiny bald nose were showing, and sometime between 12:30 and 1 a.m. Christmas morning 1945, as Orion rose alleluias in the south, while the Dipper poured glory from the heavens and Polaris remained, as always, at peace, Jesus of Oregon, calf of Peanuts, was born in a boneyard, while a boy watched and wondered at the ways of the world.

But the wonder was shattered immediately as the little wet form fell to the ground, slipped on the frozen bank and plunged down onto the thin ice at the bend of Prairie

Creek. The ice cracked and broke and he sank, in the first moments of his existence, into the frigid realities of life on this earth.

How I got him out I don't exactly recall. I do remember that the little bit left sticking out was warm and very slippery. And I remember the warnings about the danger of being on the ice screaming in my mind. He was heavy, very heavy to drag out of the ice hole and up the slippery bank, and I remember Peanuts great head at my shoulder, mooing concern and encouragement, but wise enough to stay off the ice herself. When I returned him to her feet she was at his nose in a flash, cleaning out the passage for the breath of life with the instinctive genius of eons. Within the hour he was wobbling to his feet and hunting randomly for the cosmic teat, while I returned to my family bearing tidings of great joy.

It is Christmas Eve 1980 and I am still madly at it, surrounded by the debris of creation, coffee cups — filled with hot buttered rum — over-filled ashtrays and piles of rejected pages. Somehow I feel I must finish this to share with my friends and family on our Christmas Eve together.

I live in the city now, and the confusion of Christmas has multiplied many times with the changing years. The crises of modern life weigh heavily upon us, and Christmas makes it none the easier to bear.

At its worst it is like the three wise men being held hostage for the return of John Lennon. But at its best it is

Christmas, a celebration above all others, and a time to remember those who have shared one's incredible journey upon this earth. Peanuts, Popcorn, Brownie, Bones and Horrible are all gone, as are Mother and Dad and the ranch. But Jesus? Jesus is still with us.

Little Brother

I remember I was playing in the pumphouse with my dog Tucker and my imaginary friend Beedn, when I heard the silver whistle Mother used to call me in. Even at five years of age I could identify the emotional tenor of the performer from the sound of the instrument. It didn't have that overblown tension that meant she had discovered some bit of mischief or was concerned that I had been absent too long. Nor was it thoughtlessly regular, calling that lunch was ready or it was time for my nap. Rather, it had that peculiarly beautiful quality that indicated something important and good was about to happen, and I leapt to the conclusion that maybe Dad was home and we were going to Marney's at the beach for the weekend. Beedn vanished and Tucker followed me to the house, frolicking with contact excitement.

Dad *was* home, and I performed my "Daddy, Daddy!" home-coming routine while Mother gently brushed off the spider webs and dust from the pumphouse. It was easy to tell they were on an emotional high.

"We have something important to tell you," said Dad.

To which I immediately screeched, "We're going to the beach, we're going to the beach!"

They only laughed, and Dad put his arm around Mother. "You're mother's going to have a baby," he said. "You're going to have a little brother or sister," and patted her tummy.

I could tell it was important to them and I loved them very much so I did the best I could hiding my disappointment. Neither the tummy nor the announcement meant anything to me except that we were not going to the beach. What a bummer.

My father was extraordinarily sensitive to children and recognized that this was the time to pay me extra attention. He took the day off from work and that very afternoon we drove to the coast for a Fatherly-Sonly time together. Mother stayed home.

During the next several months we talked about it a lot, but all I came to realize was that, ridiculous as it may sound, the baby was in Mother's ever-enlarging tummy. What was even harder to accept was that I had been there, too. Up until that time I had assumed that children came from Montgomery-Ward, like everything else. I used to examine the models of little boys and girls in the catalogue and pick out the ones I felt would be fun to play with. I was especially fond of a little boy that came with a kite attached.

The true significance of what was about to happen did not penetrate until, shortly before Mother was to deliver, we *changed my room.* Up until that time I had been downstairs next to Mother and Dad. Suddenly I was a big boy and I was promoted to sleeping upstairs alone, in the stifling summer heat with the wasps and the spooky attic doors.

Of the actual delivery I remember nothing. I stayed at my Grandmother's where I was chased and nipped by a goose and scared out of my wits by my older cousin, Jeanny, who darkened the windows on one of the vast upstairs rooms, played the *Sorcerer's Apprentice* on a wind-up Victrola and introduced me to goblins, monsters, witches and guilt. I have since learned that, unlike the agony of my delivery, Jolly came easily. That where I had colic and cried constantly for six months, Jolly was as happy and contented as a lamb. While our first meeting was carefully choreographed to make me feel important — I was allowed to hold him as we drove home — it was totally overshadowed by the fact that, at the same time, we got a new car, a 1940 two-door Ford coupe. Up until that time we had a Model A. The contrast was luxurious and striking. Not only was it curved and clean, but it had a *radio* and on that radio one could listen to *music!*

Measles

The insidiously irritating irony of it all is that given circumstances and ability, patience and hard work, knowledge, wisdom and a generous portion of good luck, one comes to see that no matter how much one knows, one never knows for sure. Gradually the pieces of the puzzle fall together, and there before us on the work table of the mind is a picture of something rather like a doughnut; a single geometric figure made awesomely meaningful by its symmetry and order on the outside, but with an unknowable hole at its center.

Reason and science have built for us a gorgeous cathedral, nearly perfect in every detail, and splendrous in its ingenuity and beauty, but housing only empty space. The summit of the mountain of physics is cold and lonely and the thin wrap of metaphysics cannot keep us warm.

Realizing this, suddenly we feel a need to go home, to sleep with our mates, play with our children, take the dog for a walk at the beach, call our mother long distance or celebrate some ancient holiday.

If it were still possible for me to call my mother ultra long distance, she would not be the least interested in metaphysics. Had the above paragraphs introduced any book she picked up, it would have been set aside in favor of *The Egg and I* or perhaps *The King and I.* For Mother metaphysics (or physics for that matter) was something that men did after dinner while she cleaned up their messes and saw to it that they felt good about themselves, strong enough to face the rigors of providing, and peaceful enough to stay put. For her, all philosophy could be divided between that which was silly and that which was dangerous, and one could never be certain which was worse. It was entirely too easy, especially for men, to "go off the deep end," and in her experience men who did that were either churchy, lonely, bitter, or odd, sometimes all four. She was determined that such a terrible fate would not befall her children. Not that she discouraged artistic or intellectual endeavors. That was fine provided one took care of the important things first — eating your vegetables, keeping your room clean, doing your chores and being considerate and kind to those around you.

A contemporary feminist might bridle at that description of my mother and think: poor woman, her true worth trapped within the cage of male dominance. But nothing could be further from the truth. Within the framework of the family, what Mother did was absolutely essential.

For eons creatures have been dividing the labor of life among themselves not by some political or philosophical system, but as demanded by the ultimate test of survival of the species. Like it or not, if it didn't work, we wouldn't be here.

Less than fifty years ago my mother was darning socks, making quilts, growing and canning vegetables and fruits, making cottage cheese and butter, raising chickens and supervising the logistics of a family that could number as many as fifteen and never less than six. What she did was so time-honored and obviously necessary to the survival of her family that she had no problems of self image or worth. Her universe was one of the here and now, the practical, the tested, and the known. She knew only too well that if she let the men argue politics until one in the morning, the next day they would be useless, cranky and hard to handle.

Perhaps you can understand then why it was that, sometime in the mid 1940s, when my father discovered that a measles vaccine had been developed and wished to have his boys inoculated, my mother objected. First of all it meant a long, tiring and expensive trip to Portland (four hundred miles across Oregon). But more importantly, to Mother measles was one of those diseases that all children get, much like teething, or bumping your head on the coffee table. Miserable as it was, it somehow strengthened you against future calamity. We were all dutifully vaccinated against smallpox and diphtheria, and, because we lived on a ranch, were annually needled for tetanus and rocky mountain spotted fever. We pasteurized our milk and we had annual checkups at the doctor and dentist. But measles? That was pushing things too far. And so it happened that we did not receive measles shots and six months later, after the initial period of first cold symptoms, then fever, then itching eyes, I finally erupted all over with little red spots that spelled for me measles. And for Mother, a test of her convictions.

I remember a kind of sinking feeling when she announced, "Now I know what's wrong with you. You've got *measles*!"

People were turned away at the door with the caution, "Hub got measles. You'd better not come in." And I remember being reassured by the fact that, after some discussion, Dad decided to continue with his plans for a business trip, which meant my measles couldn't be too serious.

I cannot recall what else I might have thought about it at the time. I do know what I think today when I am beset with one of the hundreds of aches and pains, injuries, illnesses and organisms that come to plague us, karma-like, as if in payment for the pleasures of living. If I caught measles today, first, if my aching eyes would allow, I would look it up in the dictionary and discover that the name comes from an old Dutch word, *mazel*, meaning blemish. Then I would move to the encyclopedia to discover the Rubella organism and to read of the possible complications, in rare cases death. I would attempt to rationalize my misery by marveling at the miracle my immune system was in the process of accomplishing. But all too soon my abstracting mind would come to the nut of it all — the mazel that disease presents to metaphysics, the problem of good and evil.

It is all so easy for us to laugh at people today who use evil spirits, witches, demons and sorcerers to explain natural events. It is less easy to do this when one is alone in the mountains on a dark and stormy night. And it becomes by far the most acceptable explanation when one strips away the last three hundred years of history. The pagan world is filled with a whole menagerie of mythic creatures to explain disaster and disease. But when civilizations began, finally, to see the interconnectedness of things, and made of many gods one God, this new point-of-view presented them with an awkward dilemma — why did God create evil? Much of the Middle Ages was spent attempting to answer that question. And it is probably this mazel, this blemish in the metaphysical scheme of things, that drove Pastor Charles Darwin out of the parsonage and onto the deck of the Beagle. Only then did it become clear that disease was an inevitable result of the way life developed.

Yet powerful as all this is rationally, it is weak emotionally. It still cannot answer why existence should happen in the first place, and the observer is so much a part of the past from which he came that he cannot escape the feeling of something more, something "out there." The vast majority of the world's people still think in terms of sin and salvation, reincarnation, karma, ancestor worship, astrology, and endless other non-rational systems to explain things. The millions of years before consciousness are still with us in the emotional, instinctive urges that we feel. Fear of the unknown, hatred of the different, the need for companionship, the sexual drive, the blessing of love, and the spur of curiosity — together these ancient animal mechanisms are forever at war with rationality. They are too time-tested and survival-proven to abandon, even though we may think we know better.

I must have met some of those medieval monsters back there in the measles bout, as my poor fevered mind tried to cope with the messages my out-of-sorts body delivered, for I cried out in the night. And there quickly was Mother, a cold washcloth on the forehead, a clean unwrinkled sheet, for no reason other than attention and action, and the powerful medicine of Mother's smell and touch. This is what she did best — caring for her child with both reason and instinct. Caring perhaps even more than usual, since it was her decision, vis-a-vis vaccination, that had brought me to this state.

But care though she might, I got sicker and sicker. There may have been an element of stubbornness involved, Mother not wishing to admit that she had made a mistake. In any case it became more than she could handle when my nose started to bleed. The nasal eruptions of measles and the fever combined to make standard remedies useless. Finally she called the doctor in Enterprise, who asked for my temperature, and when she took it and it was over 106 she lost her cool.

Only now do I realize what she must have felt, alone on the ranch in mid-winter, with three children to care for and chores to do, Dad on his way out of the county to sell hay, and me sick by what she must have felt then was her doing.

The cosmic element functions at all levels of existence. Random appearing events can, in crossing paths, become highly meaningful. Within the vastness of creation it is only chance that a planet should occur exactly the right distance from a star to allow water to exist in liquid form. Through the action of many diverse and unrelated happenings certain molecules fall together to form proteins and life. The apes develop brachiating arms to swing in the trees and pick fruit, but a change in climate forces them into a new environment where the weakened forelimbs dictate upright walking. This frees the arms and hands for more complicated activity and a premium is placed on intelligence. *Presto accidento*, self-consciousness.

History is filled with random events that come to shape its course — sea battles that were won by a change of the wind, the meeting of minds and lovers, assassinations that failed or succeeded, miscalculations that proved to be right. And always the ever-present effect of disease upon destiny. What if Mozart had lived to be 57 while it was Beethoven who died at 35?

The path-crossing that occurred in my body back there in Eastern Oregon in 1944 was an uncommon complication with measles, namely pneumonia. It was masked by the respiratory involvement of the normal course of the disease and it was, before the advent of penicillin, very serious. Aware of this, and sensitive to the fact that asking my mother to drive the many icy, snowy, dangerous miles from the ranch to the hospital in her present emotional state was asking too much, Dr. Scharff ordered that the ambulance should be sent out.

Glad as she must have been to know that help was on the way, Mother must have faced at that moment the horrible specter that, if anything happened to me she would never forgive herself.

I in the meantime had my own specters to fight as the heat of the fever melted the thin wall between the real and the unreal. Faces appeared and left, things happened to someone somewhere, sounds that I recognized, yet could not name. The bed was wet and sticky with the surrealistic red of my nosebleed, but I could no longer follow the reasoning necessary to allow things to be shoved up my nostrils. At the center of my mind a tiny black dot appeared and grew gradually larger, like a black hole, sucking in everything, until I was absorbed by myself.

Sleep and wakefulness are such ordinary states that we rarely have cause to examine them. But in fever and dreams we come to understand ourselves in a different dimension.

For there, like a hallucinogenic state, we can see that what we call reality is entirely a matter of the mind. The illusions and delusions, phantoms and fantasies, monsters and magic that the deranged mind creates are every bit as real to our perceptions as are atoms and electrons. It is a random rearrangement of the mind so that intuition can rule unfettered by reason and knowledge. In these perceptions lie the key to madness and to genius. How many great ideas and works of art may have been initially conceived in the tossing, turning, sweating misery of fever?

While I was laying there learning lessons three through six of "states of consciousness," Mother decided that this had gotten to be too much — she needed Dad. And hoping he had stopped in Enterprise before leaving for La Grande, she called the sheriff, Dick, and asked him to locate Earle. Dick found Dad outside Wallowa and sent him speeding back to Enterprise. Such are the advantages of a community where everyone knows everyone else. But there are other elements of a small town that are negative — medical facilities, for one, are primitive and ill equipped. And then there are those facts of country life that are neither good nor bad, but eccentric. The ambulance was not one of those red and white science-fiction creations with flashing lights and sirens, but a long, black somber vehicle meant to have final dignity — it was the hearse.

Imagine then what I felt when I half awakened from my fevered confusion to find myself in a world of white light, covered by a sheet, with strange voices all around, the bed canted at an odd angle, and rocking like a boat on a lake. In spite of the pain to my eyes I had to see, and pulling the sheet off my face I found myself in a blizzard of snow, surrounded by strangers bearing me toward a hearse parked in our driveway. Whatever they thought, I knew I was not dead, and I hurled myself off the stretcher into a bitterly cold but beautifully real snowbank in our front yard. This seemed to upset these specters and they began pursuing me with such obviously evil intent that Tippy joined in the fracas to protect me if possible. He held them at bay long enough for Mother to come flying from the front porch to rescue me from myself.

"It's all right honey, we're just taking you to the hospital."

It was the first time in my life that I was in a hospital, and looking back nearly forty years at the experience I am startled at the changes. The building was an old gray stone thing that had been, I think, the high school around the turn of the century. The huge high-ceilinged wards were cold and drafty and furnished only with beds and bed stands. There were no monitors, no call buttons, no X-ray, no lab, two doctors in town on call only, one RN, three aides, one for each shift, a housekeeper-cook and a school janitor who moonlighted. There was, of course, no business office either, and the fee was probably twenty dollars a day. Except perhaps for an emergency appendectomy or tracheotomy, no surgery was performed there. So for the most part, this hospital's business consisted of the dying and the being born.

I remember very little about my first day there. I am told that sometime that evening, after repeated tries to stop my nosebleed, they cauterized my nose. Which sounds terrible, but I cannot recall it. I know that early the next morning a Piper Cub from Portland arrived with penicillin, which was administered in those days through needles of giant diameters. I do remember that more because of the needles than the fact that it probably saved my life. Within twenty-four hours my fever began to drop, and forty-eight hours later the pneumonia was licked and I was left with only measles.

Measles and a subtly transformed mother. For somehow my little fandango with mortality had made a mazel in Mother's mind. An irritating, out-of-place idea that forced her to dig deep into the assumptions that governed her life. It was obvious that her unconsidered folk-wisdom was wrong, measles was not just a childhood disease. It had taken ambulances and airplanes, police and pilots, doctors and drugs, tubes and wires and needles and knowledge, and all those things that came from men of intellect and ideas, all to save her son. Suddenly those scheming, dreaming conversations in the front room after dinner no longer seemed so silly. It was there that the men dreamed up better ways to put up hay, better ways to irrigate, better ways to run a government, better ways to think about the things that needed doing. It was there that they saved babies.

Furthermore, as she told me years later lying in her own bed dying of cancer, she actually missed what she thought annoyed her beyond reason, that incessant pounding of the piano that I did whenever possible. To fill the void she had put on our old 78 rpm no-fidelity record player the only classical piano music we owned, Rubinstein playing the Tchaikovsky B-flat. Perhaps it was the worry over me, or the guilt, or perhaps it was just the right time in her life, but there, for the first time her ears were opened, and through the hiss and the scratches she heard two fine old Russian gentlemen tell her that there was nothing wrong with writing music or playing the piano. That it was every bit as manly as driving a tractor or making money. And she promised her God that if I returned she would never complain again. And she didn't.

As I began to recover, my days in the house of healing became ennui, dreadfully boring. Mother and Dad visited once a day but Mother had the other children to care for and Dad was busy running the ranch. Reading was proscribed because of my disease, and about all I could do was lie there and stare at the drab ward, or out the window at the snow-covered winterbound colorless town. But I did have one source of entertainment.

Because I had an infectious disease, I had been placed in isolation, which was, amusingly enough, the maternity ward. There were no mothers with babies at the time.

In a small town like Enterprise, there are ladies who, because they have little else to do, become professional visitors. To entertain themselves they periodically go by the hospital giving to the old and the dying the news of the day, and giving the mothers a chance to show off their incomparable newborns.

My one source of pleasure was yelling at them as they came up the stairs to my wing, "Get out! I've got measles!" They would pause, then shuffle back down, no doubt wondering what had become of the maternity ward. All except one, a tiny bent figure who must have been in her nineties and was so hard of hearing and dotty that my caution had no effect. On she came, cane in hand, shuffling across the room like a figure from Hans Christian Anderson. She stared at me for a moment.

"Whose boy are you?" she yelled in that loud voice that tells you they are deaf.

"I've got measles!" I yelled back.

"Who?" she said, undaunted. I gave up.

"EARLE MILLER," I said, as loud as possible.

She paused for a moment, thinking. "You live on Prairie Creek," she stated, and it was true. She was not totally out of it.

I nodded. "Have you seen Arthur?" she asked. I didn't know any Arthurs and I shook my head.

"What's wrong with you?" she asked.

So I summoned up all my strength and tried one last time: "I'VE GOT MEASLES!" I screamed, enjoying the chance to yell at an adult.

"What?" she said again. I pointed to the red spots decorating my arm. She examined them carefully. Then she smiled toothlessly. "You've got measles," she said, and then laughed a kind of silent gasping laugh that came from the core of her soul, and was impossible to resist, as if measles was the silliest thing she had ever heard of. I smiled helplessly back.

For a while she tottered around the room, alternately chuckling and muttering sayings that had passed for expletives in her day. Things like "Land sakes . . ." and "I'll be . . ." and "Well, I never . . ." Finally she reached the window and, staring out at the frozen town, lost her train of thought.

"Jesus loves you," she said after a while, as if talking to the whole world. I shrank into my pillow, expecting a Sunday School lesson, but that was it. Then she hobbled back to the bed and poked me gently with her cane. "You're a good boy. You'll be all right." Then, having accomplished whatever it was she was after, she made her way back to the head of the stairs and there, returning to her own private world, left me with this final request:

"If you see Arthur, tell him Pete wants to talk with him."

I never saw her again.

I have never forgotten her, and I feel strongly that it was important and that I must tell you everything as it happened, despite the fact that I have no idea what it might mean.

Who was Arthur and what did Pete have to tell him? Who was the little old lady, for that matter, and what was she laughing about?

I'll never know. Maybe it's not part of the rational doughnut at all, but rather part of the unknowable hole.

But maybe, just maybe, it was one of those random events that will someday, in some mind, cross paths with another of its own kind, and begin there an intuition, an idea, a significance, a meaning, a transformation of nothingness into the dough of rationality. Like a single Rubella virus entering the bloodstream of a child and creating there a whole universe of mazels.

To us it is a pest, to it we are a paradise.

Ranch Life

Every morning early in the bright summer sunshine or the dark frozen winter, his father woke him with his alarm-clock voice: "Daylight in the swamp!" he would say, or sometimes sing the tune, "Enjoy yourself, it's later than you think." And the boy would get up, dress, have a glass of orange juice, and go out to do the chores.

When he was little there were little chores: take one of the dogs and bring in the milch cows, Peanuts and Popcorn; fill the water troughs in the summer or chop holes in the night-new ice with an ax in the winter; ration out feed to the animals — meal and grit to the chickens, oats to the horses and cows, slop to the hogs. And if it was not mouse season, a little fresh milk to the wild kitty-cats that lived in the barn.

As he grew, so did his responsibilities: bring in the horses and harness up a work team, load a wagon with hay from the shed and pitch it out again for the hungry animals, relieve Peanuts and Popcorn of their bulging bags and carry the heavy milk pails to the house, where he would pour it through soft cloth filters, some for drinking, some for separating, some for souring.

If it was a school day, Tabasco had to be brought in, fed and saddled for the journey over the hill and across the valley. Or if it was a day for working in the fields, the equipment had to be gassed up and greased, or perhaps just a wagon loaded with wire, staples, fence posts and fencing tools. If it was a busy season, there were many people about, each with his appointed job, calling out questions and answers, laughing with running jokes and morning camaraderie. But many times he was all alone, moving by habit through the morning routine, awakening gradually like the day around him and reflecting on whatever crossed his mind.

When he was not in school, there were often things he could do to help with the jobs at hand. Like standing his horse in a gate while the cattle were separated, letting only the right ones through. Or driving the team out and back, out and back, as they pulled the hay stacker up and down, up and down, while the big people loaded the stacker with hay, or moved the hay atop the stack with pitchforks. Sometimes he delivered things, water for the thirsty, parts and tools for the disabled, messages. When the work at hand was too heavy or too skilled for him to join, his father might assign him jobs to do by himself. Some of them were fun, like riding out across the rangeland to check on this or that, stock grazing, water holes, salt licks and fences. Some of the jobs were not so much fun, like cleaning out the cow barn or the chicken coop, or piling wood or fence posts. Some of the jobs were the same jobs boys and girls do today, like emptying the garbage or mowing the yard, but with a difference. For the yard was fifteen acres and was mowed with a team of horses or a tractor. And emptying the garbage did not mean taking it out from under the sink and putting it in the garbage can. No, he had to hitch up a wagon, load up the full cans and containers from the house and the barn and the machine shop and the cook house, add to it the piles of scrap and leftovers from various events, take them all up the lane to the garbage dump, unload the wagon, wash out the cans in the creek, and return them all to their assigned locations.

With horses to ride and tractors to drive, he didn't miss roller skates or a bicycle. With all those pitchforks of hay and armloads of fence posts to wrestle, he didn't need the exercise of ball games.

There were times on the ranch, just like anywhere else, when there was nothing to do. Times when the crops had been planted and were growing, the cattle were out on the range eating, the buildings had been cleaned and painted, and the equipment readied for whatever came next, times when one must wait for the rhythms of nature to catch up, times when the weather had closed in about them and simply staying warm, dry and alive was enough. Times when it was dark out early and though dinner was over it was too soon to go to bed.

These were the times when they took vacations, when they left the ranch with someone else to milk the cows and feed the stock, and visited friends and relatives out of the county. They might go to Moscow, Idaho and visit the Cushmans, where they could eat strange food in a Chinese restaurant or watch a college football game. They might go the long four hundred miles to Portland where he could pound on his grandmother's piano, ride the streetcars and check to see if the outrageous stories his cousins told were true. It was here he got to see movies or very special things like the Ice Follies, church, or a full symphony orchestra. Some of the things they did in the city were not always fun, like the doctor and the dentist, or, strangely enough, going to the zoo. Seeing those poor animals all penned up forever, many of whom he knew from home, seemed cruel and selfish.

Sometimes they would pack horses into the high mountains, the Wallowas, where the boy could fish for trout, pick huckleberries, and explore the land of ice and snow. Up there he saw deer and elk, mountain sheep, a few bears, and once even a timber wolf. Once they got snowed in and had to lead the horses out by hand. And on one of those trips they lost a horse, Cimmeron, who, having been raised in the flatlands of Arizona, became terrified on the precipitous trails and jumped to his death.

Once a year there was Chief Joseph Days, the annual county rodeo, when the town filled up with Indians, cowboys and tourists, and everybody got drunk and did things that they only did at this one time of the year. The boy remembered how fine it was to ride Tabasco in the parade, how he once won the junior division cow cutting contest, and how he over-ate at the cowboy breakfast and then threw up riding the Octopus at the carnival. It was great fun.

But sometimes things were quiet and the boy stayed on the ranch without other children around. At these times there was reading. When he was small his parents would read him things like Aesop's fables, Hans Christian Anderson, *Alice in Wonderland*, or around Christmas, stories from the Bible. Later, when he began reading for himself, there were all the Nancy Drew and Hardy Boys mysteries, and longer, harder books like *The Jungle Book*, or his favorite, *Green Grass of Wyoming*.

There were some books on his parents' shelves that fascinated him, and he read at them even though he could not understand them fully. One was Nostradamus, which was about predictions an ancient man had made, many of which seemed to have come true. He would read a section and then later that week things would happen just as Nostradamus had said: the Allies would invade Europe, or the President would die. But just when he thought he had it figured out, when he was certain that there would be an earthquake tomorrow, no earthquake would come, not even a thunderstorm. Then there was one book that was very, very hard to understand, but was probably his favorite book of all. It was called Paleontology, and was about the bones of animals that had lived a long time ago. There were many drawings in it of dinosaurs and trilobites and fossil shells, one of which looked very much like the fossil shell he had found while exploring at Hurricane Creek in the mountains.

If the weather was nice enough to be outside, a lot of his time was spent making things. The tools and raw materials were readily available and making things was much more common than buying things, partly because there were no stores around to buy them from, and partly because many of the things one imagined or needed could not be bought.

One of his projects was the marble track. This one began when the boy found some ball bearings left over from some long discarded transmission or rear end. They were heavy and rolled smoothly and invited invention. He rolled them down an old wooden flume that had once carried water. He rolled them down some sheets of corrugated tin roofing, then laid the sheets together so the steel balls passed from one sheet to the next and then into the flume. But the real break-through came later that day when he saw the garden hose. What if you laid two lengths of hose together, side by side? Would they not make a perfect track?

And there was plenty of hose around, old hose, new hose, hose used for irrigating, and hose used for spraying the cattle for flies. The trackway had to be carefully engineered so that the hoses stayed together and the heavy ball bearings did not drop through. They could be banked and turned, run uphill and downhill, or even jumped, as long as each section was tested and redone and tested again so that the speed of the rolling bearing matched the characteristics of the track. Too fast and the ball would leap off, too slow and it would stop. Loop-de-loops were designed, switches and alternate tracks put in, tunnels, bridges and all manner of excursions much as you might expect from a model railroad. Except that it was done by gravity.

At the end he placed an old steel beam that rang like a bell when struck. Many weeks were spent enlarging the project until the hill behind the house looked like a miniature golf course, with boards and bricks and lengths and lengths of hose. For a time, not a hose on the ranch was free. Even the cowboys and ranchhands, many of whom liked to pretend they were too old for play, enjoyed the ball bearing project.

Then one day he was rummaging around outside the machine shop and came upon a pile of discarded electrical parts. Knobs, dials, switches, transformers, batteries, parts of old cars and radios. He had no idea what many of them did. Laying there rusted and rained-on and waiting to be taken to the dump, they spoke to him a fantastic message: a lie detector. All the rest of that afternoon and several of the days that followed, the boy was busy about his secret project with such intense industry that questions were asked.

What the hell is he doing?

Of course, when finished it didn't actually work, but it looked fantastic. Lights flashed, motors hummed, dials glowed and needles wiggled, all controlled by his ingenious deceit.

He tested it as usual on his little brothers, always the first to be included in his fantasies, and then on one of his visiting cousins. So successful was the device that they were totally taken in. He tried next Mrs. Mac, the cook at the ranch house, and then his grandmother and finally, the ultimate test of an undertaking, Mom and Dad. They laughed, of course, when he told them about the project, and when they first saw the unlikely machine. They became somewhat more concerned, however, when wires were wrapped around their wrists and attached to terminals X and Y and when the DETECTO CROWN was placed upon their heads. "You sure this won't shock me?" they asked.

The interesting thing about it was how gullible they all were. How, even though they knew better, they couldn't help wondering sometimes, when the results came close to the truth, just what was going on. A question would be asked, an answer would be given, and the lights would flash and the needles jiggle as the boy's own intuition would search through what had been said, the body language that accompanied it, and all the subtle unspoken things he had learned about animals and people. And then, buzzzzz, the buzzer would sound — they had lied! His mother was an easy subject, she rarely lied, and when she did, it was obvious. His father however was tricky. For although his father could play the game better than anyone else, he had an obligation to see that fantasy and reality did not overmix. Furthermore, here was as fine a chance as any to instruct his son in true scientific method. So his father saw to it that the sham in the operation was exposed, but in such a way that only he and the boy knew it. All in all, the lie detector was an immense success.

For friends he had plenty. There were the adults, who were usually happy to teach or tease or talk as they went about their work. Children his own age visited from time to time, especially in the summer, sometimes staying for weeks — cousins from the city with unbelievable stories and dangerous ignorance, and ranch children like himself who traded visits for mutual company. When friends were visiting, it was a festival of fun: hide-and-go-seek in the old barn, building forts in the baled hay, day-long excursions to his special places: the eagle nest in Pinetree Canyon or the cave in OK Gulch, and nightly explorations of one another's feelings and secrets.

But mostly his best friends were the animals themselves, for he loved them greatly, and shared with them the joys and sorrows of growing up. From their quiet wordless ways he learned much of their wisdom and foolishness, and saw reflected there his own.

Many miles of trails were covered talking to Tabasco about the things that crossed his mind. Where did we come from? Why are we here? And though Tabasco didn't say much, his horsy ways were full of answers: the surefootedness on steep mountain trails, stepping carefully but naturally around rocks and badger holes, the instinctive fear of the dangerous — some of it imaginary — the need for companionship of other horses and men, and the way he traveled faster when headed homeward.

Sometimes when things were not going well for the boy, when he had lost his favorite pocket knife, when he had been punished for something that he did not feel was wrong, he would lay his head against Peanut's warm flank in the morning as he milked and listen to her advice. The rhythmic munching of her cud and the gurglings of her many stomachs spoke of an immense motherliness, of patience and acceptance of one's lot, and of giving freely and giving again.

He spoke to tadpoles and caterpillars about growing up in general, to weasels and magpies about cleverness and deceit, to eagles and coyotes about killing and death.

And the trees told of time past, and the rocks told of time long past, and the stars told of time itself.

Lessons

As a child, I was a klutz. I can laugh about it now that my hair is gray and falling out and my bones ache when the weather is changing. In fact, I am even thankful for all the rejection those early missed catches and wild throws produced. I was tall and strong and bright and fast; yet, had I not also been a gangling uncoordinated sissy, I might well have invested my soul in this body that crumbles around me.

My lack of skill at sports brought about my first confrontation with maya, illusion, in our culture. And though I lost, I won.

Back in the 1940s, when I was coming of age in rural America, sports were, if not everything, cruelly important. Looks meant nothing, grades meant nothing, money meant nothing, unless you were also on the team. And I was not. For the most part I could pick my friends only from others like myself, the late-maturing, uncoordinated disabled, which included the retarded, the neurotic, the insecure, the minorities and occasionally a "normal" who was just a newcomer. I was lucky that my father understood this situation, probably because, with our common genetic heritage, he had, when young, experienced some of what I was going through. After a few games of catch with his oldest son, he realized that I was much better suited to riding a horse or a tractor, which I did well, or reading a book which I did prodigiously. For the rest of my relatives, peers, and acquaintances, sports was the common meeting ground, the American way, the measure of ability, and the prime indicator of future success.

Perhaps as a by-product of this shortcoming, I was born with an immense talent for music. There was no reason for this, no past relatives, no present influences. In the canyons of the Snake River about the only music was the songs of the birds, the wind in the trees, and whistling. We did have one of those little wooden gothic-arch radios which, with an antenna strung on the roof, could extract from the morning air the Inland Empire Farmer from KHQ in Spokane, and thus the current prices of cattle, wheat, hay and hogs. Their theme song was the Sons of the Pioneers singing *Tumbling Tumbleweeds*, which sounded to me then like the *Hallelujah Chorus*. On Sunday one could hear Jack Benny play the violin and Dennis Day would sing. And once in awhile on cold winter nights the earth was magically changed as there drifted in and out of the ether fragments of great symphonies from a civilization long ago and far away. During those times I was enchanted into stone before the tiny speaker.

Four hundred miles away in Portland my grandmother had a piano. When we visited, I spent as much time as I was permitted discovering the intricacies of the keyboard. By the time I was five I could play short pieces of my own invention with such authority that my parents were forced into a certain responsibility toward my musicality. They were able to get for me a Kimball reed organ, one of those highly carved, church-in-the-wildwood species common in early America, and I pumped my way into the future with music as my guide.

During the half dozen years from six to twelve, none of this mattered much. I did my chores and went to school and joined in the activities of the ranch and county much as everyone else. When I was free I made music by myself. But as puberty approached, the gulf between myself and my peers began to yawn. Their sporting skills increased enormously, while mine did not. My repeatedly flubbed plays were laughed at, and being chosen last for every team began to hurt. My jock relatives would take me out to the horse pasture and bruise my fingers and feelings with interminable baseball throws and catches, or sadistically instruct me in the fine art of self-defense, while the time I spent with my music was suddenly resented. "Why don't you go out and play like the rest of the children?"

Today one can carry a guitar down the halls of a high school with pride. The bad boy Beatles and Rolling Stones are marching at your side. The popularity of romantic rebels would soon arrive, but in those days it was either play ball, or odd ball.

I was not, however, a totally lost cause. I could run well, swim well, ice skate well and on a horse I was a natural. At the rodeo sports, roping, riding and cutting cows, I was a match for anyone. I could back two wagons through a gate with a tractor. I could usually talk my way out of fights. And I was extremely good at cutting up in class and generating pranks.

And slowly, slowly, neurons were connecting. Once in a while I caught an important pass, hit a hard grounder, or made a long shot basket. It wasn't much, and it wasn't often, but it was enough for me to keep hoping to change slightly my picture of myself, to just barely be able to enjoy it.

And then a miracle happened. Through a combination of underpopulation and injury, the Joseph High School basketball team, in the middle of a winning season, was reduced to seven boys, and I was asked to join. All I had to do was provide a little relief for some of the real players, but I was needed and I was on the team. For four weeks I actually played high school basketball, and what I learned from the experience has been of profound value to me all my life.

Make no mistake, I was awful, ridiculous in fact, the ugly duckling, a species removed from my teammates. I made few points and gave away hundreds. I had no idea what was supposed to be happening in any given play and would more often than not find myself exactly where I shouldn't be, either alone while the others played it out elsewhere, or blocking my own teammates' progress. The crowds laughed at me and even booed and hissed, and I can still remember opposing team members standing on the sidelines scratching their heads, not believing what they saw.

In spite of my play, we won. For a combination of cosmic reasons, which no one understood, my presence on the team caused a quantum leap into a universe of basketball where the normal, the ordinary, and the expected did not apply. First of all, my teammates, recognizing that they had a non-entity aboard, were charged up to play their very best. Secondly, just when the opposing team figured out what was happening, and started to ignore me, I would, quite by accident, do something right. Thirdly, much like the function of the clown at the rodeo, the temptation to watch my ineptness distracted the bulls just long enough to give my team an advantage. It was rather like playing chess with an opponent who moves at random: they had to figure out if my moves had some significance.

I was totally honest with my fellows about my inadequacies, and they were good enough players to exploit them. After some of my blundering *faux pas* were enigmatically transformed into scores, they began to smile and wink at me, and a strange thing happened — we began to like each other. When our coach, after the second game I played, read me the riot act, with the best intentions I am sure, I was startled to see my teammates spring to my defense. “It worked, didn't it?” they said. Gradually some of my more successful goof-ups became established sucker plays that worked again and again.

Having been an outcast for so long, it was a role I had mastered. The basketball court became my stage and the game my performance. When, after a month, the injured real players returned, I was not asked to leave the team. I only played then after we were far ahead, but I played and I improved. We won the local league championship.

Other things happened, too. Suddenly many of the peers and teachers who had ignored or ridiculed me wanted to be my friend. I was too polite to rebuff them, but I could not forgive them their narrowness. And now that it could no longer be considered sour grapes, when adults approached me with sportsy-wortsy jock talk, I felt free to make my true feelings known. “I still prefer music,” I said. But in truth it did mean a lot to me; and although, being a fish out of water, I could never really enjoy it, I did bask a bit in the sunshine of fellowship.

But I had one more lesson to learn from this affair. It began on a morning when we were scheduled to go to La Grande for the Eastern Oregon Class B high school basketball playoffs. Even if it was only as a mascot, I was proud and excited to be going on this adventure to the big city

(La Grande had 10,000 people!) as a member of a winning team that represented my acceptance into manhood.

Spring comes late to the high country and the ground had only recently thawed. A few green shoots of grass and wild flowers were poking up, but it was too early to plant. We had no beef cattle yet, and the registered cows were up on the range calving in the clean peace and quiet where they do best. During this fallow period, the hired hands were on vacation, resting before the storm of spring and summer work. Even Dad and Art Harsen, our foreman, were away in Weiser, Idaho, buying steers. Mother and I and my little brothers were alone on the ranch, and I was up early on that cold, gray morning, milking Peanuts, feeding the horses, filling the water troughs, working quickly to finish in time to leave for the game at La Grande.

Early that morning a Piper Cub buzzed the house and when I went out to see who it was, a rock with a note attached dropped. It was Dad who, as was his custom when having been away, had taken a plane from Joseph to give the ranch an overhead survey. The note said, "Hub. There is a dead cow in the dam. Take a horse and see if you can get it out. I'll be home late this afternoon. Dad." By the time I read it the plane was gone. It was seven and a half miles up Pine Tree canyon on a horse to the dam, and there was no way I could do both the game and the ride.

By the time I got back to the house I was in tears, ranting and raving. Mother agreed with me that Dad, having been away, had forgotten entirely about the tournament. And yet, there are some allegiances and realities that go beyond feelings. Dad had asked me to do it. I was the only man on the ranch. It was important; a carcass could pollute this vital source of late summer water. And worse still, I knew that, for all my feelings, the team could get along without me.

It seemed as though this was the worst thing that had ever happened to me, and it was a long, cold, bitter ride through the bleak, snowy, desolate day. Everything went wrong. The carcass was hard to approach because of the rotting ice. When I finally got one leg snagged and pulled, my saddle slipped, which sent Tabasco into a frenzied, bucking, panic. Then, because the carcass was so waterlogged and heavy, when I finally got a good haul on it, my seventy-foot braided rawhide lariat, a prized cowboy possession, broke. Finally, in my anger, I had run off without lunch.

As I started home, I was a stormy sea of crossed purposes and confused loyalties. I hated my father during that ride as only a disappointed fifteen-year-old son can, and over and over I rehearsed the terrible things I would say to him when I got back.

As the afternoon wore on and the distance shortened, the flurries of wet, friendless snow tapered off and then stopped, the sky began to brighten, and shafts of sunlight struck the distant mountains. The birds came out to celebrate, busy about making up for lost time. A great blue heron startled my horse and me into being here, now, seeing the ever-present wonder of life. And the fatigue and accomplishments of the day began to calm my feelings.

When at last I crested the hill that looked down into the valley Prairie Creek had carved, and could see the little cluster of buildings and trees that were my only home on this earth, I could also see Dad riding up the lane to meet me. And from the wave of his hand alone I could tell everything: How very badly he felt about his thoughtlessness, how very proud he was of the job I had done, how very much we loved one another. In fact, in that short ride down the lane back to the barn, Dad and I were as close as we would ever be. Not much was said, but a great deal was communicated.

We took care of the horses and went directly to the house where Mother and the boys were waiting. And suddenly it was Christmas. We were celebrating some kind of family something that was beyond words. Rituals were needed. Dad offered me a drink for the first time in my life, and I accepted: scotch on the rocks (that's what he drank). It tasted awful, but I drank it with as much casualness as I could fake, and it had the desired effect.

Mother had a good dinner waiting and we all sat down together and exchanged our experiences of the day. Dad had bought seven hundred head of steers to be delivered from Ukiah and they would arrive next week. Mother had a war with the washing machine, which I promised to fix. Jolly (ten) had spent the day cleaning the machine shop and had found a rat's nest. And Lee (seven) did one of his improvised, indecipherable monologues which were family famous for their fun. It was easy to feel that though the wide, wide world might knock upon our door with either gifts or bills, it could never come between us.

Then, at eight in the evening, twelve hours after the rock had fallen from the sky setting this day apart, it struck again. This time with a different, heavier message. The phone rang and Dad answered it. We could hear him say in that overly loud sing-song voice he used on the telephone, probably a leftover from the days when phones barely worked, "Hello? Yah, this is Earle. Oh, hi, Dick, how are you?"

And then "Yes?" But this one simple word in a suddenly lowered voice. A voice we knew only too well. A voice that meant something serious, something uncomfortable. Even the little boys recognized that voice. Suddenly the room was silent. Mother looked concerned and my mind raced to catch up. Dick? Dick who? Dick Rawlinson in Portland, one of Dad's best friends.

"Well gee, Dick, he's right here with us . . ."

He? It must be me.

"Yes, Dick, umm, we had an emergency here on the ranch and I had to keep him home today."

My mother could stand it no longer.

"Earle, what is it?" But my father only gestured her to be still.

A long pause.

"Uh-huh . . . Oh, my God!" His voice quivered and my mother moved over to grab my hand. I think she guessed already.

Dad continued, "It's a hard job you have, my friend. God bless you. If there is anything I can do . . . Yes, I will. Good night."

Dad sat on the sofa, his hand on his forehead, staring between his knees as we waited.

Finally he looked up at me, tears welling in his eyes, and said in a strange, scratchy, constricted voice, a voice torn to the North by sorrow and to the South by thanksgiving, a voice I shall never forget, "They were all killed . . . All except Tom Eagleston . . . And if he lives he will be totally paralyzed. The car went off the Minam grade in a snowstorm. They didn't find them until five this evening."

This is not a romantic French novel where the facts can be adjusted to milk the emotions. This happened just as I have told it here. It punctuated in unforgettable italics my grandmother's oft repeated homily: everything works out for the best. From that day forward, all the petty disappointments in my life, the broken promises, the hurt feelings, the leaky faucets and flat tires, all have seemed but blessings in disguise, gentle reminders of this long-ago lesson. There have been other happenings in my life with other, different messages to tell, some happy, some awesome, some sorrowful. But all alike in this sense: that suddenly, for no reason, accidentally, the pieces of the material world fall into such a pattern as to speak, irrevocably, a seeming spiritual message. No heavenly choirs, nor even still small voices in the wilderness. But only the normal everyday whirling of the universe as seen through the lens of understanding.

I draw no theological conclusions. I do not feel that it was "meant to be." It is no more, and yet no less, miraculous than existence itself.

Yet I do wonder sometimes, I cannot help asking the question in my heart of hearts, why me? Do these things happen to all men? Are the messages not there for all to read? Why are so many men, my teammates on this planet, lost? Lost in the work-a-day world of short term profit, in the tit of primetime pap, in the butcher's block of prejudice and hate or in the swamp of self pity from petty, meaningless disappointments.

I was asked to speak at the memorial service for my teammates, but I chose instead to play. My father trucked into the Joseph High School gym one of the few decent pianos in the county, a Baldwin six-foot grand. There were over a thousand people there.

It was the first time I had ever performed as a musician in public outside of family gatherings. The piece I played for them went like this:

I began with an up-tempo rendition of the Joseph High Fight Song, replete with octaves, drum rolls and piccolo riffs. Then, midway through the third phrase, I interrupted it with a sudden giant chord out of whose resounding there grew, in a new and unexpected key, a pianissimo arppegiated base figuration, much as you would expect from a Chopin Nocturne. Over this, through many chromatic harmonies, unusual yet satisfying, I wove the fight song theme again, slowed down by many orders of magnitude and ornamented freely. Occasionally there were short counter melodies in the depths of the bass, and near the end was a pianissimo cadenza that explored the uppermost registers. Ever retarding, it resolved itself finally into forever.

Journey Home

From 1942 to 1957 (my seventh through twenty-second years) my address was Double Key Ranch, Joseph, Oregon. Although I was born in Portland and vaguely remember the mild, wet coast, it was there in Wallowa County that my roots set down. It was there I learned to live on, off and with the earth, that if I cared for it, it would care for me. It was there, in the shadow of Joseph Mountain, that I learned the basic laws of living with other men and women; take care of yourself, help others if you can, if you can't, leave them alone. It was there on the banks of Prairie Creek that I learned to doubt and question; that there were many different ways to put up hay, that laws made in Salem or Washington were often meaningless or disastrous in the land of the Nez Perce, and that what was true for people in Enterprise was not always true for people in Imnaha.

And it was there, from Jidge and Tommy, Reverend Stover and Silvertip that I learned to have faith. That no matter how late, spring would come; that perseverance, patience and good humor could finish the hardest of jobs; that even if I was stuck in the snow at midnight, miles from anywhere, the moon on the mountains was magic and eventually someone would show up to help me.

My story is common enough, perhaps the most basic American experience, in many ways the story of man. From out of the canyons I came, riding a horse, resourceful and tough, but naïve and limited. Into the green valley of agriculture; hay, wheat, small towns, high school football games, Saturday night dances at the lake and Chief Joseph Days.

There I learned to work and play, plant and harvest, read and write, get drunk once in a while and fix anything with baling wire. During that time, right after the war, the horse gave way to the tractor, the pick-up and the car; the chemistry of 2-4-D and DDT promised to control pests and the first sprinkler systems began to hiss their way onto the dry land. The first house was built at the foot of Wallowa Lake (by Max Wilson's son, if I remember correctly) and most important of all to me personally, we got a piano and I had my first lessons from Jean Jacobs. I have been a professional musician all my life.

But all too soon the needs of education and the wanderlust of youth took me away. I went off to college where I learned how Wallowa County fit into Oregon and the Pacific Northwest; what it was like to live in another climate where water was taken for granted; what it was like to live in a city where nobody knew who I was, where people thought boots and a hat were a costume and were amused when I said "howdy" or "slaunchwise" or even the words creek and roof.

And the car gave way to the train and the airplane, and I was off to California and New York, London and Katmandu. Learning how Oregon fit into America, and America into the whole world; where a white shirt and a tie were as foreign as cowboy boots and hat; where not a word of English was spoken; where to be a Christian was to be an Infidel . . . arkidesh . . . pig-eater.

Had it not been for music, I would have returned to Joseph, Oregon long ago. To live in that special place on this planet that I love the most, and to pass on to others the values and truths that I have come to trust and honor — Wallowa County ways. But just as a piece of land must be used for what it does best, so a man's inner soils must be plowed and harvested with the crop his talent dictates. And yet, though I have been away, the concerts I play, the music I write, the ideas I pursue and the feelings I trust are but Eastern Oregon turned into music.

Yet so many things in this life turn out to be an illusion, a far-off childhood fantasy that melts upon close examination, or a comfortable dreamland urged on you by the society in which you live. Furthermore, with the great changes that have come about during my lifetime, the enormous increase in population, the unexpected results of technology, and the flattening out of differences as transportation and communication brought us all closer together, few are the places on this earth that have not been changed beyond recognition.

So it was not without some apprehension that I returned recently to the land of my childhood, the land of my family, the land of winding waters, willing and able to accept the truth of whatever I found, but hoping beyond hope that my sweet memories were not some poetic construction of my own mind.

Together with family and dog, I left my home in Seattle under gray skies and crossed the state of Washington, spending the first night at Palouse Falls and the next day visiting friends in Moscow and Lewiston, Idaho. For anyone who remembers what that drive was like thirty years ago, it was a staggering experience. Gone is the wild Columbia canyon twisting its tortured course toward freedom. In its place is a sculpted reservoir tamed to serve. Gone are the vast stretches of nothing, sagebrush and coyotes, sand and sky, that spoke of eons of untouched time beyond memory. In its place a miracle of man's making, water pumped, crops raised, highways blasted, atoms split, every inch owned and fenced and posted and very much used.

Gone are the little lonely towns, oasis-like, tucked in a hollow to hide from the sun and the wind and the vastness, with a tree or two, a grain elevator, a school, a church and a store. In their place are modern service centers, motels and RV parks, Denny's and Mastercard, or, like the tri-cities of Richland-Pasco-Kennewick, whole chunks of Los Angeles transposed. Nothing I have read or seen about where man is at today on the earth as a species has impressed me so vividly, so tangibly, as this three hundred miles. Depending on your perspective, you may see this as a great challenge realized — food to feed the world — or a dangerous cancer of population out of control.

Somehow growth in the cities, for all the problems it brings, is an irresistibly exciting thing. Great buildings soar as statements to wealth and power. Hordes of diverse people rush and bustle, mix and melt, and test out new things and new ways. And though it is noisy and dirty, confusing and even dangerous, it remains civilization at its peak, where merchandise and medicine, parts and products, art, ideas and entertainment that we *all* use are created.

But growth in the countryside, though reason tells us it has to be to keep us fed and supplied with raw materials, exacts a terrible toll in terms of the balance of things. Gone are the open spaces, the free places, the earth as it has always been. And we are forced into accepting how totally interdependent we all are in a system of technology operating at its limits. All these things I considered while driving down the Lewiston Hill. The new highway is faster and safer, a blessing I am sure to those who must drive it often. But it is not as much fun, it is not as beautiful, and the Snake, that once wild river, is a lake.

But coming up the other side out of Asotin and across the top to Anatone, things begin to change. It was the same old road, twisting and winding and making right angle corners at sections if need be. There were no cars coming, no sprinklers running, no buildings unexpected, no jolting reminders of thirty years gone by. And as we dropped into the Grande Ronde, back at last to the canyons where I came from, the real canyons, there was the river, slowly making its natural way as it has for the last million years. And the little store at the bridge was still the little store at the bridge as I began to climb toward home with a song in my heart.

Because it was so perfect there, and because it was getting late, I decided to stop and spend the night, and just where the road makes that U and begins to climb in earnest, I parked the car and carried the sleeping bags up the creek a hundred yards, just inside the Oregon border. As good a place as any, I felt, to experience the canyons again. I know it was probably illegal, and to whomever's land it is, I apologize, but somehow I felt I had the right. The last time I was there was with my father, when our truck froze up with a load of cattle, and we spent the night moving around to keep alive.

It was difficult to get to sleep. The excitement of travel, the hard ground and the sea of memories were churning up inside, but by one a.m. I dropped off, dreaming of Buckhorn and Aneroid. At two-thirty, just as the moon was rising over the hill, Wallowa County made it's first move when the dog discovered the porcupine. Oh, there was much yelling and yelping and an exaggerated aura of crisis in the night as we dug up a flashlight and pliers and I pulled out quills (all but three). And I did feel sorry for the poor dumb city slicker, learning his first Eastern Oregon lesson. But inside I was bubbling with a kind of childhood joy: it's still here, it's still real, it hasn't changed.

Recognizing that we would likely not get back to sleep, we packed everything back in the car and headed on into Enterprise for more comfortable lodging. It was a blessing to watch the first pale dawn over Joseph Creek and enter the valley as the first golden light touched the peaks.

There is no need here to describe everything I saw and did, everyone I met or everything I felt. But I would like to hit a few of the high points.

I went first to Chief Joseph's grave at the foot of the lake, the most sacred place in the valley and probably the most beautiful. I cannot forget that we took this land from them by force. And while history has taught me that it is the way of the world for the strong to take from the weak, I cannot help but feel that our spirits are now intermingled, that by living here in this land we have become more like them than they like us. I went also to the pioneer graveyard by the Joseph airport and put old history together reading inscriptions: the infants dead of smallpox; the twenty-one-year-old son lost in the First World War. But mostly it was sprawling lilacs knocking over the tombstones as life goes on and all things are forgotten. And I wished that my bones could lie in so lovely a place.

I went to the Wallowa County Museum, something new yet not new, and found there a picture of Liberty School, which was on the corner of our ranch and where, until it burned (two days before school was to start), I daily rode my horse to learn the three Rs. And sometimes at night we would sneak over and throw stones at the teacherage, a cowardly act but required of all respectable young ruffians. How many kids today have their school closed for a week because of a skunk or a hornet's nest?

I drove everyone with me crazy pointing out things that meant much to me but nothing to them. There's the Craig's (I remember when Guy married a Southern Belle). There's the Dobbins' (I remember how long and honorable was the blessing at Sunday dinner). There's the Dorrance's (Tommy taught me to braid leather and broke my first horse). There's Max Wilson's old office. And there's where Walter Klagas beat me up.

I visited the hospitals in Enterprise. The old one up on the hill where I was in the maternity ward when I had pneumonia and measles at the same time, and the new one, twice as big, where Dr. Scharff brought me back to life after I broke my neck in a logging truck accident. And next door, in the Enterprise Community Church, I was moved to tears remembering Joyce Best singing and Edna Craig playing . . . the first live music I ever heard and the first place original music of mine was ever performed. To honor his mother, who was a great teacher, I bought a straw hat from Don Jacobs at the Enterpriser.

I dropped by and visited Doug Tippet and his family briefly. He looks and sounds just like his dad, thank God. And although we were never close, and he doesn't realize it, he was my childhood idol — oh, that I could be like him!

And finally I visited the Hough's at our old ranch and was delighted to discover what fine people they are and how glad I was that they were living there. There, in the very house that I can first remember Christmas, in the barn lot where I first got bucked off, amidst the very things from which I learned the deepest lessons of my life, I learned anew — that this house, this barn lot did not matter. That it could just as well have been up or down Prairie Creek ten miles, or out in Billy Meadows or Cold Springs. What did matter was the mountains, the valley, the canyons, the people and the way of life. Wallowa County. The long winters, the isolation, the laws and the integrity of its citizens had kept it whole and healthy. It has not changed at all.

Oh, there are little things here and there; a new school, a few apartments and motels, better roads, more irrigated pasture and some newcomers manning the tills. But the guts of the place are still vital and real, like a porcupine, simple but lasting. And the spirit is alive and burning just as it has in my mind for so long. Few men today can return to their childhood for so rich a reward.

Then all too soon it was was time to leave for Seattle and home, and as a parting gesture we went to the Wiggins Lodge at the lake for a drink. There it was, exactly as I remembered it, with a kind of class and quality almost vanished from the earth. Downstairs in the bar, with memories of mother and dad, Jidge and Jesse, Bob and Janet, Tabasco and Trigger, almost all gone now, I read a most beautiful sign on the wall which stated far better than I can the philosophy of Wallowa County that I have lived by happily all my life. I did not have my writing things with me and I would not dare to paraphrase it, but I recommend to anyone interested in a good life to read and follow its advice.

Finally, like pinning the tail on the donkey, like the coda of a symphony, while walking around the lobby reading the brands, there I discovered ours, and my father's name. And I hope you can understand why I felt right about signing the guest book Hub Miller, Double Key Ranch, Joseph, Oregon.

BLACKBERRY

But as with so much knowledge, it was there in the dark quiet unused areas that the real truth lay.
It is 1952 and I am eighteen . . .

Blackberry

Rubis ursinus (Pacific), laciniatus (Evergreen) or more likely procerus (Himalayan) is one of the most successful niches yet discovered by life evolving. Ubiquitous to the wetter parts of the world, it has founded in the Pacific Northwest a horticultural civilization of vast proportions and high achievement. Depending on your perspective, inclination, maturity, character and mood, it can be described as vicious, pesky, common, green, sweet and (dare I say it) loving, and I will admit to having had intimate relations with it on each of these levels.

Like many species, Blackberry reveals itself to us in a variety of forms: the fragrant blossoms are beautiful, the thorns are painful, the fruit is sweet. It is impossible to get rid of. In fact, until recently man has had neither the scientific knowledge nor the emotional fortitude to perceive the Blackberry for what it truly is. But as with so much knowledge, it was there in the dark quiet unused areas that the real truth lay.

It is 1952 and I am eighteen. I have come to Seattle from across the mountains where it is dry, dry, dry, where the necessity and blessing of water is still understood, where civilization has scarcely touched and a man can trust to his own resources; where the spaces are wide, the cowboys lonesome and never, never a Blackberry has grown.

I have found my first home away from home, a quaint, seedy red and white houseboat moored inconspicuously under the University Bridge.

In the joyous throes of that first pubescent clean-up, fix-up, paint-up orgy that is common to new tenants, I encounter (and as I see now quite providentially) a vast network of some weed-like plant occupying what small moorage area I have that lies above water.

"That," I say foolishly with my mind's eye on a world that will never be — perhaps a world of grassy slopes with flowers and pretty girls, or a practical world of peas and beans, or maybe a poetic world with birdbaths and sundials — "That will have to go!"

There on the banks of Portage Bay was a dense cluster of intertwined vines rising in great gothic-like parabolic curves from some central point hidden by their own profusion. The scope of this particular infestation was roughly fifty feet on a side, the major stalks about an inch in diameter, branching frequently but randomly, emitting slightly smaller versions that repeated and repeated in ever reduced scale. All portions of the plant wore some form of thorns, testament to their rose family lineage. The thorns varied from hard, half-inch major weapons on the larger stalks through smaller eighth-inch versions on the branchlets to tiny babies cradled under the center vein of each leaf and finally a harmless cilia-like fur covering the leaf surfaces themselves.

Armed with my ignorance and a pair of household scissors, and with no vague hint whatsoever of what was about to happen, I approached what was to be a major branching in the vine of my life. I did not know that first gentle tendril would lead back eventually to the root of all things, that it would be a virgin encounter with otherness that transcended my as yet unconsidered metaphysics, an initial prick of a thorny truth that would brand me forever as a man and only a man, that would draw the blood of a beast beyond this place in the scheme of things and infect me with a slow but irrevocable poison that would lead to my enlightenment.

I leave out the tears, the sweat and dirt, the failures, the waiting and the trying again and again with other different manifestations that would eventually give this first encounter meaning.

Like all the information and misinformation pouring into my head up the hill at school during those days, it would take years to settle, to mix with chance meetings, strange people, unplanned events and unexplained phenomena. It would need to be leavened with love and loss and luck. It would need to ferment by means of some cosmic yeast that will never be fully explained, having to do with why we are here at all. And finally it would need to resurface, transfigured.

This description is a synthesis of all the Blackberry Wars I have fought, win or lose — clearing campgrounds on the coast, rebuilding my brother's greenhouse, searching for lost hub caps, raising flowers and vegetables, painting or repairing outbuildings, helping friends move and other sleazy histories. I include here certain shady gullies of the mind where I explored and found twisted thickets so like the thorny creepers of the "real" world that I cannot say for certain which is which.

My response to this initial encounter with Blackberry was, I think, "Son of a bitch!" which is Eastern Oregon for *voila*, or in proper British, "Oh, dear!"

Though I was understandably ingenuous and uneducated at the time, I was not stupid. It took only a few snips of my scissors and pricks of my fingers for me to recognize that my initial estimate of this undertaking had been underrated. I was quickly reminded of the wise counsel to care for number one first, which seemed to dictate gloves, long pants and heavy boots. And like the hands of Homo sapiens, there is no substitute for the correct tool.

Shrouded in protection, I return to my purple patch armed with the weapons of the field: shovels, rakes, pruning shears, elbow grease and determination. I clip back some of the forward scouts. I reach back into the dark, dangerous guts of the beast searching slowly, cautiously for a major artery and severing it with my shears. Then I pull, harder, then harder still until at last either some soldier spine breaches my gloves or I manage to extract this wounded individual from the mob. Occasionally this tactic works, and I can add one more fifteen-foot tentacle to the pile growing behind me. But more often the intertwined, multi-branched individuals hang on to their friends and neighbors, linking their thorny octopus arms and clasping their many vegetable fingers, acting under, I soon come to feel, a pre-Pleistocene treaty of mutual defense, to resist, *en masse*, the assault of this upstart biped enemy.

It is my first tentative sensing of Blackberry's social behavior, and I am impressed.

Then I come, in the middle of things, to death. For, unlike most human cultures that see death shortsightedly as an ending, in the Blackberry world it is clearly manifested as the central issue of the living. No sooner do I unbutton Blackberry's green outer garments than I find brown and rusted, bent and brittle, yet still quite dangerous, the tattered undergarments of some past existence. As the remnants of some ancient berry village are revealed, my college digs become suddenly archeological. Arched ribs that once lived here peacefully under some younger sun, a dried-out, faded skeleton that must once have furnished scaffolding for prehistoric spiders. The shells of musty pioneers stalked this spot and claimed it for their own long before the advent of houseboats and students. Without them these green flyers of today would not be half so high. It is these relics that first tilled the soil here, that fought back the ivy and won, that shaped the basic patterns of this patch and they that, till my onslaught, bore the weight of the living.

With this discovery I am faced with a new dilemma. For though I am literally sophomoric at the time, tactlessly proud of my new-found agnosticism, more than ready to rip into ritual and religion with the rapier of reason, though I am newly unshackled, I am not wholly amoral.

The burial ground of ancestors echoes some deeper taboo and I feel the tug of forces I thought I had overcome. It is one thing to exhume Materialism in a dry, warm well-appointed academic study. It is entirely another to make one's bed in a graveyard on a dark and stormy night.

So under the pretext of taking a break, I stop for awhile, have a cigarette, a cup of coffee and survey the damage I have done, progress I have made. I laugh at my misgivings and rehearse the arguments until the act seems trivial. Then I return to work, less a conquest of reason over superstition than a matter of mere momentum. I discover that in death these stalks are even more terrible. Brittle and hard, with thorns that detach easily, working their way into my clothing and scattering about the ground to be discovered months later by bare feet.

I reach ground level with the sun and find gnarled tuberous roots running down and out in all directions, headed by grotesque ganglia from which the stalks emerged. I find broken bottles, cans, mildewed junk mail, plumbing parts and rotting boards and I see how this seemingly useless bramble was, in fact, a handy hideaway: a headline from the 40s, a few collectable bottles and a rusty but ringable bicycle bell. And one truly valuable find, a sign from the bridge above reading PROCEED WITH CAUTION. It will go on my bedroom wall.

It is fully dark before I am done digging, scratched and dirty, tired, but curiously alive with that macho rush that comes with a heavy job well done. It is Saturday night and I shower and scavenge the refrigerator in preparation for the Blue Moon. There I will drink pitchers and schooners, tell my life story properly exaggerated if not wholly invented, and solve the world's problems by means of the next election. Maybe Karen will be there.

Early next morning I will return, properly drunk and disorderly, with just enough presence of mind to note the extra blackness I have created there on the bank. Sunday noon I will awaken feeling "not too bad, considering," and coffee cup in hand I will stroll onto the back deck to survey yesterday's victory. Only then will I realize that I have only moved Blackberry several feet. Somehow that huge and painful pile of dangerous debris will have to be moved again — to the dump this time. And am I mistaken or have the boundaries of my cleared plot not shrunk a bit? Was that one long creeper there yesterday?

I wish I could answer those questions yes and no respectively, then, having covered Blackberry extensively from fruit to root, make an end to it. But in fact I have, if you will pardon the expression, barely scratched the surface.

For — and this is one of my major discoveries — there is no end to Blackberry.

I made of my clearing there on the bank as much as was practically possible. Grass and flowers grew, but not nearly fast enough to survive without my constant intervention. I did raise a few green tomatoes for the slugs and I found it a convenient place to store my rowboat. But a sundial seemed almost as foolish there, where no sun struck, as did a birdbath by the edge of a lake. And had a pretty girl lain down on the mouldy, slime-covered, sticker-ridden aftermath of my labor, I would have shunned her ever after.

I did not do much better in my academic pursuits at school. By the time I had cleared away the brambles of chemistry and physics, I found for the most part a kind of rooty mind that was gnarled and twisted by blind faith in rationalism. Profit and position entered into the equations as a kind of hidden constant. Knowledge was deemed valuable for its own sake, and if there were problems inherent in the application of medical, chemical and nuclear technology, those were for the humanities to consider. Up the hill where fiefdoms of the humanities jockied for position, the sciences were viewed with effete disdain, endeavors fit only for one-nut bastards who kept the machines oiled. In history the real story of creation was filtered through minds that could still believe, *carte blanche*, in the destiny of man — reminding us again it was the 1950s.

There were two realities, and the one that took place "outside the department" was eschewed. The School of Music had inbred to produce only two acceptable periods of consideration: the Baroque, which was enjoying a revival at the time and marched under the banner NOTHING SINCE 1750, and the modern, which had lost its teeth chewing on the experimental, its claws to the cerebral and thus weakened protected itself by pushing the myth that Beethoven wasn't appreciated in his day, either.

Far, far from this precious world was romantic music, beloved of the masses and thus considered beneath contempt, and popular music, still patently drivel, although, unnoticed at the time, folk music and amplification were humping in the wings, about to give birth to an off-spring destined to populate the future.

I learned far more that year in the halls of Blackberry than in the Halls of Ivy. For despite it's common, ugly, brutal ways, at least the vine was demonstrably real, a rare quality in those times. It must have been amused at my novice attempts to play Man, the Invincible Ruler. After all, what were a few paltry twigs to that mighty species? But somehow, in spite of my wicked behavior (like a naughty child in need of a nap) she must have loved me. For while

I was snipping and tearing and pulling, unaware of where my mind was drifting, she planted therein a tiny symbolic seed that would sprout in the spring and send thorny tentacles out to connect all things together.

It began as an improvised joke when, while describing the afternoon's employment to friends, I propounded the not inconceivable and to me amusing theory that there was only one Blackberry vine. I called it Monster Mother Blackberry, playing on the phrase Seattlites applied to the Boeing Company. Patches, I claimed, were only just visible manifestations of a single giant organism all interconnected underground. To support this hypothesis, I proposed a kind of vindictive behavior where, while you were trimming back one place, she was growing out another. This seemed most reasonable to fellow Northwesterners, who were quick to contribute supporting testimony. The internal seed had germinated.

I was gone for the summer, back to the ranch to earn my keep, and when I returned to continue school I found my backyard largely reclaimed. It was fall though, and the vines were laden with sweet ripe berries. Partially because of this gratuity, but more probably because I had some accurate idea of the effort versus the reward, rather than trim it all back again, I moved the rowboat and used my energies to have an unhappy romance. All in all, it was not half so painful, and much more nourishing. The neighborhood ducks took to roosting in what clearing remained, providing entertainment from my kitchen window, and the dark scar I had created began to look natural again. Perhaps this softness and sensibility on my part would have happened anyway, but more likely it was the first symptom of symbolic runners stabilizing my brainstem.

I did much better in school that year, not because conditions had improved, but only because I seemed to deal with them better. I no longer looked to the University for answers to questions but rather for questions to answer. I saw it now for what it mostly was: an obstacle course designed to exercise those skills needed to perpetuate the American Way. If one could negotiate registration, endure fussy details made overly serious, feign interest in pet dead-ends, stimulate foggy graduate students well suited to research but unfortunately teaching for their keep, ignore power politics of the ivory tower hierarchies, and meditate on institutionalized boredom, then one was prepared to advance into the world of corporate business and industry.

Paradoxically this lessening of commitment to *alma mater* only improved my grades and increased the esteem of my peers and teachers, while at the same time releasing great gobs of time and energy to my own personal extracurricular budget.

I learned to savor the pleasures of the home, and there, with Monster Mother's gentle guidance, to flow with the currents of the season. All that cool gray winter long, while she slept dripping on the bank, I lollygagged and dawdled, reading, playing the piano, studying the surface of the water as it waved at passing boats or made circular smiles at the rain. And when it grew cold and still, as fog enveloped the bridge and the boat, I knelt on the dock like Narcissus and studied my own reflections.

As spring brought us back to life, Blackberry probed the space and light around her patch with long, thin, green investigations, while I explored the city on my bicycle, visiting relatives, both man and vine. To keep from being wounded as I passed, I was forced to trim back the trail that led from the dock to the road, but she seemed not to mind, being busy in the patch I had surrendered. By June she had it completely reclaimed and burst into blossom to celebrate. Taking her cue, I blossomed also, bursting at last into the world of adult relationships, and was fully occupied until the school year ended.

That summer, back on the ranch, my parents found me considerably changed, and fretted a bit. Soon I discovered that lollygagging and dawdling, when observed, become brooding and malingering, an annoying clash in the style of that vigorous environment. Their shy attempts at understanding my altered demeanor met with uncalled for resistance. My random reports of what went on at college in no way supported the myths they entertained: fantasies about football games, fraternities, learned lectures and flashing but practical insights. I felt exposed under the clean, blue empty Eastern Oregon skies, as if the damp, dark, delicate cultures germinating within me would soon turn to dust and blow away. I felt estranged from the very earth that had nourished my childhood, an urban alien left behind on some unmapped primitive planet. After the lush, green populous coast, the people seemed amusingly quaint but shallow, the hay and wheat docile and domestic and the sagebrush simpleminded. I tried on the suit of local behavior, but it no longer fit. My cowboy hat had become a costume and the sweet homey smell of barn on my boots a lingering reminder that my past and my future were falling apart. The closest I came to friends that summer was a clump of Canadian thistle that crowned the hill behind the house. There I would go after dinner to smoke, to collect my other selves together and to draw from the thistle's lonely windswept tenacity some courage and support. By August the thistle had dried up and died, but not without sharing with me a message in the millions of fluffy parachute seeds that happily took to the frivolous wind, unguided and alone, leaving their home and blowing away as part of some larger plan.

Perhaps it was the same with me. Perhaps those silent summer sadnesses were no more than growing pains, a matter of tissues and enzymes, species-specific behavior and enculturation, that notch in time's arrow where it becomes necessary to box away childhood, like grandmother's soup tureen, and remove it to the attic. There it may lie, unused, unmissed, until some very special occasion calls it to mind — a wedding, a birthday, a wake. Or more likely, amidst the rush of becoming a man, be forgotten completely until some time, years later, while adding insulation in the attic, it is rediscovered (by chance, we like to say) untouched by time, yet filled to the brim with savory nostalgia. Perhaps, perhaps, perhaps. I will grant these qualifications to those who demand of their metaphysics totally sanitized materialism.

But I feel strongly that it was more than that: that it was, in fact, Blackberry, solidly rooted below my surface, and sending her green stickery arms out in all directions searching for the light. Then, having found the light, casting a symbolic shadow of ever-connected-oneness against the nearly white wall of my emerging consciousness.

Returning to the houseboat that fall for my last year at school, I found a totally transformed world. Monster Mother had built upon her patch a veritable Taj Mahal of horticultural architecture. Drawing upon the resources of connections at the bank, she sent fleet runners to bridge the gangplank and feed festoons of rich vines that embroidered the railings of my deck with baroque abundance. Berry-born seedlings had sprouted in the window boxes to jail the pleasant pansies behind bars of thorny wildness and squeeze the marigolds into dark ghettos. From there she began her search anew, climbing up to drink from the gutters, following out the cracks between boards and diving towards the deck like green fountains overflowing. One very precocious vine had probed the missing pane in a bedroom window, and finding a desk, had curled comfortably around my Websters Collegiate Dictionary like some scholar's cat. There at that symbolic book of words, where language has its safety deposit box, where the grunts of beasts become the mind of man, where being and meaning dance their ephemeral waltz, there the material manifestation of Blackberry ended. There at the very spot where, accidentally or providentially, my own internalized vine began.

Through me that tender young reaching crept out of the bedroom and into the kitchen, out the back door and across the gangplank, up the trail, across the bridge and out onto the hill where the University was institutionalized. The image of a complex, yet ever connected living oneness, provided for me a skeleton upon which I could hang the many disparate facts and details that crossed my own climbing. The cold numbers at nine a.m. math were but symbols of the pressure, volume and temperature of ten a.m. chemistry. These in turn were modulated by the accident of biology at eleven and created history at one. From there the vines would blossom with the flowers of philosophy at two; delicate and attractive illusions, where the future came to be by the random mixing of molecular ideas. Later, in the Commons with my coffee, many of these matings came to naught — hothouse freaks too weak to live amid the wildness of common sense, pseudoberries that danced on the head of some medieval pin ignoring human nature, or crossings whose results were magnificently utopian, but sterile.

Many more there were that bore real fruit. Common everyday facts and figures to fill the lunchbox of life: tax laws and typing, statistics and style, how to calculate the angle when sawing boards or chairing meetings. Much of it was purely decorative — fancy phrases in foreign tongues that were, in fact, graceful street-language, plus a whole arsenal of names, quotes, references and syntax that communicated more by class consciousness than content, and allowed one to seem comfortable in an intermission clutch of lobby literati for whom such class was everything.

But amidst all this there was real nourishment. History, the tangled stories of all those dead and brittle vines hidden beneath our present patch, began to make some sense out of what had always before seemed a curiously random shape. The mountains and valleys, rich thickets and barren empty places were but reflections of the past, the residual effects of floods, droughts, pests, competitors and many, many long lost years of peaceful growing-out and dying-back to the rhythms of the earth. Reserved and frozen here for me to sample, and protectively packaged by the University's isolation from the needs of the community at large to profit materially, were the rich harvests of other seasons, other vines, other reachings toward the light. Jars of poetic jam to spread upon the bread and butter of data and add to it the sweetness of understanding. Bottles of aged purple wine to celebrate one's communion with everything. And, most important to me personally at the time, a new family to supplement the weakening ties with my own almost accidental flesh and blood connection. For here, scattered haphazardly about the shelves and store-rooms of recorded time, were the pickings and recipes of brothers and sisters, mothers and fathers, men and women who would become my larger, lasting family: the family of man. The family that civilization was storing in my mind. They, too, had fought with thorns and brambles and lost, then reconsidered and contemplated and finally come to live in peace with, indeed, to love Blackberry. They too had been touched by some common weed and found there to their amazement a cosmic connection.

If you have read this far you have probably sensed the romantic demon in my nature. You can probably guess that my last year at school was a delightful fugue of academic fantasy. Charged with the energy of youthful discovery and connected at last to the real university, the library of all human knowledge, I became a novitiate in the monastery of the mind. Casting behind me the temptations of lolly-gagging, dawdling and other earthly pleasures, I hurled myself with zealous devotion at what I then considered to be the scholar's way, a frenzy of acetic excess. It was not without its value.

For though I lost my color to the dusty pallor of a basement carrel loaded with seldom opened books, books that tended to be visibly esoteric . . . Egyptian hieroglyph, Latin poetry, pre-Devonian paleontology, Icelandic myth, tables of numerical lists. Though I lost some friends to the pedantic certainty of my trivia or the seeming lack of commitment that comes with too much cultural relativism, though I lost the social benefits of my fresh Eastern Oregon charm, still I was gaining some purchase on the mountain of material that must be climbed to experience an overview. Bit by bit, tale by tale, I was researching the story of how I came to be me, the story of man, the story of life, the story of creation. In this tale, against the total scheme of things, Blackberry and I were scarcely more distant than cousins.

If in this *Gradus ad Parnassum*[1] I was lost to the details for a time, it is understandable. There are an infinite number of them. The fetal mind is as grotesque as the fetal body, yet, given time and luck, it can become a thing of beauty. It can also become a monstrous freak. I hear it often boisterously babbling in collegiate coffee shops or confidently addressing conferences on esoteric subjects, or ranting and raving at political rallies. It is a kind of mind that finds within the walls of words a hole in which to

1. Gradus ad Parnassum is a seminal textbook on counterpoint written by Johann Joseph Fux in 1725, but used well into the 20th century in music instruction. "Doctor Gradus ad Parnassum" is a satirical piano composition by Claude Debussy poking fun at Fux's exercises. —wls

hide, a tidy, punctual type of thinker who trades the challenge of totality for the comfort and security of specialization; or a skillful technician who screws in one innocent part, unconcerned that the end product is war; or the wild man who studies his subject intensely that he might not see himself. Oh, yes, there is a Siren singing in the study halls of schools whose endless, well-made melody will fill our ears with the words of others until we cannot hear ourselves. By springtime this wili[2] had coiled her snaky charms around me, warmly oiling my ear with a soft incessant whisper that seemed to say:

Here now my child is your real home at last
Amid the sacred scribbles of the past.

But it was not to be. For Monster Mother Blackberry had, in her unfathomable creeping, invested in me some portion of her earthy magic. She was not about to sacrifice this investment to so ephemeral a phantasm as mere knowledge. I shudder to think what might have happened had I imprinted on a more permissive plant; the thornless blueberry, for example, willing to grow in rows and play domestic. Or the mushroom, already well adjusted to living off the light of others. I might well have rooted there amid the stacks as resident idiot savant, a shufflemaster in

2. Wili, Slavic creature of folklore. For the English-speaking world, the wilis are usually associated with the Romantic ballet *Giselle* by the French ballet and opera composer Adolphe Adam, first danced in Paris in 1840. Its spectral wilis are young girls who have died on their wedding days, who almost snatch away the hero's life-breath, but must disappear at the break of dawn.—wls

academic slight-of-mind, a biological reference room so weighted down with words that I could not run the mile of thinking.

As I lingered late in the library those days, slurping at the froth of facts, the thorny lady-by-the-lake missed my loving attentions and reached out to restore the connection. Gently she laid reminders across my trail. But I, returning home in the dark of night with a crowded consciousness forever fogged with thoughts of elsewhere, I would dodge her probes with bicycle art, or cruelly crush them beneath my tiredness. Or when they finally scratched at my body, stop to clip them back, unaware of their motherly message. Undeterred, and cleverly sensing my obsession with words, she then wrote across the kitchen window one great circuitous sentence of Blackberry syntax, the herbaceous equivalent of chicken soup nagging, no doubt, that sought to trim my mealtime view with a viny admonition to enjoy, to rest, to live in the present. I noted this new encroachment vaguely, at the commas and semi-colons of my tasteless convenience meal. I found in it only an amusing addendum to my stylishly beatnik abode.

My table was set in those days as a still-life of the very disproportion that hobbled me. A dirty plate of cold canned something or other and a carton of milk, surrounded by a choppy sea of books propped up on crusted sugar bowls and ketchup bottles, note pads trimmed with chili droppings and cornered with buttery encounters, the silverware transformed like Cinderella's midnight into pencils, pens and rulers, and the whole composed to achieve an effect of long-established disarray. Peering through the window at the pale, ill-kept, red-eyed, self-entranced creature that had created this tableau, Monster Mother must have telegraphed a new urgency through her many far-reaching departments. My own biological mother would have bridled indignantly, called me by my full name, and in a tirade of despairing love set about the penance of housework.

Blackberry moves in larger, slower circles, having at her disposal deeper more ancient elements. During the night, a wind arose and rain began to fall for the first time in weeks. The glorious spring that the suntanned student-body had celebrated was interrupted temporarily as great oceans of wet arms swept in to wash the blood, cool the tempers and balance the energies. The houseboat creaked and groaned, confessing to the waves its mortality. Rain played a raga of metrological music across the instruments of the earth: rolls on the tympani of the roof and the cymbals of the water; atonal woodblock xylophone tunes dripping at the ends of the eaves and the sills of the windows; glockenspiel tings and triangle tangs where glass and metal performed their garbage can sonata. The rigging of seldom-used sailboats whistled their eerie loneliness off to the wind and rumbled their bumpers in protest. And here and there unexpected virtuosi emerged for one night stands: a

Best Foods mayonnaise lid filled with screws on maracas Español, while a spike in a floating railroad tie moving across a discarded wood stove delivered a rusted recitative of wretched *Sprechstimme*[3].

It was all a ruse, of course, called up by Blackberry to cover the rustle of her creeping and to touch me at that one connection where I am most vulnerable . . . music.

I could not sleep. I could not concentrate on today's accomplishments nor plan tomorrow's agenda. The cleansing energy of the storm and the uncanny beauty of the natural concert touched chambers in my mind too long ignored. Against the intricate accompaniment of this cosmic orchestra, I recalled to my soul the familiar song of Home on the Earth, and as I sang, tears formed in my mind as I found there loneliness. The great castle of civilization shuddered as my fingers fumbled in the dark at its foundations and felt there nothing. Searching through the storehouse of recently accumulated facts, I sought an answer, a reason, a meaning for these feelings and was shocked to discover not a hint of help. The empty house mocked my needs and its gross disorder and filth reflected

---

3. Recitative and Sprechstimme. Sprechgesang (German for "speech song") or Sprechstimme ("speech voice") is a technique of vocal production halfway between singing and speaking. Since the end of the 19th century, it has sometimes been called for by composers of classical music. Recitative, a form of composition often used in operas, oratorios, cantatas and similar works, is a melodic speech set to music, or a descriptive narrative song in which the music follows the words. It is used where dialogue or monologue is sung in between the arias, choruses or other numbers, and is intended to help move the story along quickly. — wls

my inner disarray. Early in the morning the wind died down, the rain stopped, and when the dripping had diminished to lullaby levels, I half slept, half dreamed, vaguely aware of another soft sound, not quite knowable.

I awoke to find the storm over and the sunshine returned. The trap of habit directed my momentum, and I planned to return to my monastic quest. Waiting until Saturday for housecleaning seemed a reasonable compromise. Blackberry, however, had other plans beyond the niceties of moderation and good behavior. The face that her five-point eyes had found at the table the night before had set her roots, stiffened her arms, sharpened her nails. Her pride injured at the fickleness of my love, her dander raised by the danger she saw and her veins coursing with the strength of the storm and the emergency message from Grandmother Ocean, she grew in one short *Walpurgisnacht* a mammoth and intricate Blackberry barrier to block my egress beyond her patch and dispense a kind of primitive justice where *habeas corpus* is hocus pocus, bail and bribery are both denied without hearing and trial by torture is recommended.

The weight of the wetness upon the branches that had once soared high and dry now bent them out and over and down to close the trail with a gate of a trillion glittering teeth. For insurance, the runners that had used for their youthful purchase the slot where the gangplank attached to the deck had grown and swollen to make the slot a non-slot, so that the action of the night waves sent the gangplank adrift somewhere out on Portage Bay. Finally, should I have felt manly enough to row to school, by some monstrous magic I will never figure out, the rowboat was no more. Sarcastically slipped through the ring where the bowline had once been tied to the deck was a tender young vine of the species Rubis procerus.

I did not for a moment question that this extraordinary outgrowth was a willful and vindictive yet wholly natural act on her part directed at me personally, and I cursed her and stamped about the deck as befits a child confined to his room.

Already sensitized to my isolation by last night's stormy visions, I could accept the karmic instruction that accompanied this "act of God" interruption to my plans, but at the same time my species pride was injured. By collective wit, man has come to be dangerously unfamiliar with the mercy of the elements. Yet my "I'll show you, you son of a bitch!" response was ironically squelched as I could not seem to locate a pair of gloves (how the hell did she manage that?), and as I recalled with amusing frustration that, in a fit of post-orgasmic gratitude, I had loaned my pruners to the moon-eyed barmaid at the Red Robin (or was it the red-eyed barmaid at the Blue Moon?).

The impact of technology upon civilization became immediately clear as I recognized that, declawed of tools, I was hardly a man at all, that no amount of reason would breach her walls, and that on a one-to-one, Hub-to-Blackberry basis, she had me outclassed. Exaggerated as it may sound, I admit that, for just a moment, a current of real fear flowed through my nature as the caged animal searched for a route of escape and an explosion of real joy illuminated my soul as I determined that I could swim to a neighboring float, if need be, while she could not.

Closely bound to the grin that arose from this victory was a far more sophisticated sense of the absurd. One of those rare and precious Zen moments where matter and mind are brought together in a single clapping chord, where infinite pasts and futures implode on the perfect presence of *now*, where tricky illusions of time cease and being and meaning are seen as indistinguishable. The blue sky, the white clouds, the golden sun, the sparkling water and the invisible air all mingled together their joyous energies on the prismatic mirror of mind, and joining their handless hands in a circleless circle, sang together the song of eternal brotherhood. Through me It laughed at Itself. A real laugh of human bellow and lungs, yet an unreal laugh of cosmic forces erupting. An excited laugh of discovery and joy, yet a tearful trembling laugh of love overflowing. The laugh that a stranded survivor might laugh as the rescue ship approaches, the jack-in-the-box glee of a child, the soft throaty laugh of a mother first feeding her infant and the proud, brave laugh of a father sending his son off to the future.

Here in my backyard many years, later trying to record that moment, I am still rocked on a wave of profound gratitude, and glance up to salute the thorny mound of creeping green that is my local connection. I have had other moments of truth in my life, but none more timely nor meaningful. I recall that I spent the remainder of that day happily entrapped on my floating home, exposing my naked body to the wind and the sun and the moment, and confining my distractions to a half case of Olympia beer and a box of Ritz crackers. The next day I hitched a ride to shore with Tiny Tankers (the boat that delivered our heating oil in those days) and after a week of clean-up, fix-up, paint-up and a heavy bout of Blackberry trimming, I returned to my ways of lollygagging, dawdling, romance, reflection and music. With this commencement I had graduated, Bachelor of Being, University of Blackberry, Class of '55.

PACIFICA

And as the bones of our ancestors begin to mix with theirs, we feel a tug of distant brotherhood.

Golden Gardens

If you would like to tune in to the music of Seattle, to hear the dark symphony that is both her strength and her weakness, if you would like to listen to the bass line of her music, the underlying harmonic tremors of her personality, then I suggest you celebrate New Year's Eve alone out at the sandy spit of Puget Sound-side park known affectionately as Golden Gardens.

In an attempt to control summertime teenage rituals of rebellion, the parking lot closes at sunset. But mid-winter if you are man or woman enough to walk a quarter-mile on your own two feet no one will bother you. I suggest you wear something warm and waterproof, with heavy boots, for nine years out of ten it will be cold and wet. Every tenth year it may be clear, but then an arctic wind will blow across the exposed beach and yesterday's wet will be frozen on the ground. Or you may, if you are lucky, find yourself amidst a Pacific storm, with the surf foaming on the beach, the logs adrift, the rain horizontal, the temperature unseasonably warm and the darkness charged with exchanges of metrological energies. At such times the precarious position of man on the earth will be immediately clear and you will easily admit your utter dependence on civilization. Step carefully, for you will find here no boardwalks, no streetlamps, no signposts to guide you; only an empty stretch of beach quite typical of this part of the world and much as it has been for the last fifteen thousand years.

Find yourself some shelter behind an old driftwood hemlock skeleton if it is mild, or up among the scotch broom on the sand dunes if it is blowing, and hunker down close to the warm protective earth for a while and just be.

You will find little to remind you of the city at your back. The sounds will be wind hissing the bushes and waves breaking on the sand, with just a vague mournful foghorn perhaps or the thrumming of a freighter or airplane. And though the sky to the south will glow with the city's presence, and, if it is not storming, a few strings of lights will twinkle from the peninsula ten miles across the water, they will do little to distract from this cold, dark, lonely picture.

You will understand then why so many of the early explorers sailing this inland sea for the first time described it in terms of the end of the earth; an enormously complex arrangement of islands, inlets, fjords and peninsulas edged with rocks and shallow beaches, the dense and largely impenetrable forests rising from the shore in dark green cascades, growing into jagged mountains of ice and fire in the distance. It was a land that spoke to them of many difficulties and far, far from home.

Today people flock here in the summers to explore the luxurious forests, challenge the formidable peaks, and experience a natural beach and the freedom of the wild, but it is a freedom that depends heavily upon aluminum frames, freeze-dried meals, down parkas and a hot shower at the end of the trail.

As your soul settles in for this midnight vigil, as your pulse slows, your senses atune to the surroundings and the busy buzz of life today is dampened down to a distant ache, time will begin to run backwards. Your thoughts will turn naturally to the early explorers and settlers and pass quickly on to the cultures of peoples that lived here long before them. The city-glow in the sky will dim and then extinguish. The twinkling lights across the sound will wink out one by one, except for two which will become bonfires briefly, then burn out as their tool-bearing masters retreat to Asia from whence they came. For awhile the gulls and the clams and the trees and the water will be left to their own devices. But gradually the rocks beneath them will quake and shift, mountains will rise and fall and explode, coast lines will grow and recede until all is returned to the fiery ball of beginning.

Pause here briefly at the beginning of this journey and glance back at the city and you will see Seattle in its best perspective: an almost inconceivably tiny thing in terms of galactic proportions, but a miracle nonetheless — the offspring of a twenty-billion-year-old love affair between matter and spirit. That it should be here at all is annoyingly paradoxical. That it should, through you, look back in time and consider itself is awesome. You see it not as compared with other cities, but as an expression of man upon the earth. And all-in-all, it gives him a fair accounting: a glowing beacon of controlled energy shining out to the thoughtless void its messages of mindfulness and of searching beyond hope for an answer; a living seed that could, if planted on any hospitable planet, endure to reproduce its kind; an accident, they say, of cosmic dust colliding, and yet so formed as to make it seem curiously predestined.

Throughout the course of man's migrations upon this planet, several cultures of peoples have, with great difficulty, found their way here and set about the task of making this land their home. Stragglers still arrive. Each begins with a vision in mind of all he left behind and a storehouse of rules for behavior and technology that has allowed his people to endure. Yet slowly these rules begin to change, adapting to a new vision. The past becomes a nostalgic legend of questionable relevance overwhelmed by the power and beauty of the present.

Unquestionably much of this is adaptation to a new environment plus the spur to cultural evolution that comes with isolation plus the character of a people that would find this environment and this isolation attractive, indeed, necessary. But at the risk of sounding provincial, I must admit that, after years of consideration, I have come to feel in my heart of hearts that it was much more than this. That the facts of latitude, climate, biology and behavior did not fully account for the differences. That the isolation was much greater than could be explained by high mountains, impenetrable forests and vast oceans. That the adaptations that came about from living here struck at the roots of human spirituality.

Until recently I would not have written that statement. Had my romantic intuition, in an orgy of confession, put it on the page, the more rigorously disciplined scientific materialism in my eduction would have read it and quickly deleted it as being wholly speculative and tastelessly sensational, a product of my own special feelings about this spot on earth. But current reasoning in the fields of geohistory, refinements to the theories of continental drift and plate tectonics, and the bringing together of many anomalies and contradictions found amid the rocks that make up this part of the earth have revealed a possible basis in fact for these powerful feelings of unique difference. This chunk of planet is not, it seems, a part of the American continent at all, but a collection of wandering islands that sailed across the Pacific Ocean two hundred million years ago and rammed into the Canadian shield, creating devastating beauty.

Pacifica it is fittingly named, a long thin strip of very special history that decorates the western shore of the American continent.

Esoteric facts such as these mean little when trapped in traffic on the Evergreen Point Floating Bridge during Friday rush hour of Memorial Day weekend. But at midnight on January 1 at Golden Gardens, amid the rain and darkness, they are of profound importance. They balance nicely the physical measurements against the great weight of intuitive feelings that arise from living in this land. It is *in fact* different.

From midtown at midday the hustle and bustle and muscle around you may seem but a commonplace example of contemporary American urbanity. Cars and buildings, people and products, fads and fashions. Indeed, to some residents it is only that; people whose roots are elsewhere, people who, in spite of citizenship are foreigners; modern men and women who, by sad circumstances will never have a home. But to the core of residents, often with very little conscious awareness on their part, the city is but a grand illusion, an evil that is necessary to provide them with the means to live here. They are not so much doctors and lawyers, construction workers and receptionists as skiers, sailors, fishermen and climbers. To aid with commerce and communication they have learned to imitate the behavior of their continental peers, practicing business and industry with considerable success, trading the natural resources of their homeland — trees and water, fish and natural beauty — for the multinational products of the 20th century — engines and energy, information and material pleasures. But like the continent to which they are attached, some inner Western-most part of them remains aloof; the Pacifica part, as it were, of their metaphysical makeup that is not for sale — a childlike thread in their fabric that is cowboys and Indians, a remnant of hominid flesh that will not be civilized.

Indeed, leaving civilization behind had a great deal to do with this concept called Seattle. For though there is a fine example here of urban Homo sapiens, a vitality that hums by day and glows by night, an organic collection of peoples and things that is large enough to sustain its own center of gravity, its own identity, its own style, still it is a youngster, a frontier town, a postscript to continental history.

However grand the schemes of man may seem when compared with the schemes of man, here they are kept forever in their proper place by the overwhelming natural surroundings. Towers of glass and steel may seem like mighty prayers on the flatland, but here they are but matchboxes against the mountains. The hot egoistic energies of man's bloody currents are watered here and cooled to meditation. Connections with the past and visions of the future are all too often clouded over with the soft gray pleasure of the present, as beneath us ever murmurs the message of Pacifica's mindfulness.

Kah-Kah

"Dammit!"

Dwight glanced in the rearview mirror to determine if the car behind him could stop in time and flashed his brake lights defensively. It wasn't the Friday afternoon of three-day weekend traffic that had him down, but the bite of deep disappointment.

"Who the hell do they think they are?"

Swedish Hospital had just informed him that he would have to work tomorrow under circumstances that precluded escape. He didn't really mind his job in the business office and he could use the extra money. But he had been looking forward to this weekend for a long time as a chance to go out to the coast and revisit Toleak. It wasn't so much a mini-vacation as a yearly pilgrimage to a spot on the earth that had helped him discover himself. He had been promised next weekend as compensation, but that did not satisfy the equation. This weekend was the full moon, the biggest tides of the year, and a partial eclipse. Hot, sunny weather was in the offing. Next weekend the tides would be small, and with his luck it would rain.

He shook his head. His own discontent he could manage. A karma-like principal had long ago entered his life, partly learned from visits to Toleak, that had led him to an easier acceptance of events as they happened. Many times what seemed at first a bummer later turned out to be a blessing. His disappointment was one thing, Nancy and the kids another. Nancy would have the sleeping bags rolled, ice chest stowed, ferry schedule checked. She was going to be seriously annoyed. She would take this as another example of work taking him away from home, from her. Cautiously he examined her side of the argument. Was there, in fact, a better way to live?

• • •

"Nika wawa ikt." I tell you one time.

Old Three-Eyes voiced the pain in his feet from many miles of travelling rocky, log-strewn beaches, and the ache in his belly brought on by the reasons for this journey. Reasons that had to do with his being old and all but useless, and thus considered wise in the ways of Tahmonowis, Great Spirit. Wisdom his people believed was part of age and pain.

"Nika halo delate kumtux?" What does any man know for sure?

Tahoma had sent him out alone on this journey for both good reason and selfishness; to investigate tales of strange happenings at Ankutie Nauits, Old Beach, the spit of sand that marked the northern boundary of Tilikhum territory, and also to remove Three-Eyes from the village long enough to marry off Tahoma's daughter to a younger man — for fifteen blankets and *two* long boats. In a sparing mood, Three-Eyes' offer had been one boat short, and thus he would not have a new young wife to warm his bones at night. Tahoma would give him instead Meetsmeets, the skinny Quilcene slave obtained in last year's raid, an undertaking Three-Eyes had frowned upon and a squaw his other wives would never accept.

Gleefully imagining that it was Tahoma in all his Potlatch finery, and drawing upon images of whale blubber, Three-Eyes barked at a nearby boulder, "You are ugly and you stink!"

But even as the gulls laughed at his impertinence, he recognized the wisdom in Tahoma's decision. He, Three-Eyes, was too old to keep a young woman happy, and investing status in strong young men was good politics for Tahoma and the future of the tribe. Besides, at the moment he was much more concerned with what had washed ashore at Ankutie Nauits: artifacts of some strange and skillful design, made of materials he had never before seen, for what purpose he could not guess. That some of this would be of great value for the Tilikhum he could not doubt; especially the hard, red, rock-like things that did not break but bent, and the large piece of inexplicably woven gray fabric that was as light as a feather but strong as a blanket. That this strangeness should enter his world so late in life disturbed him. To maintain what little status he still commanded, he would be expected to explain these things. What stories could he invent that would strengthen and enrich his people, no matter the truth?

• • •

Finding himself alone on the sand for a moment, Dwight suddenly felt happy. How well it had all gone. Nancy had seen his disappointment and instead of pouting had helped mollify the children. Marcus and Rema had been more than happy to substitute this sunset trip to Golden Gardens for the longer, harder journey over to the coast, although some of this hinged on the promise of a Sunday movie. There, with ape-like pleasure, Marcus was scaling a log that jutted out over the rocks. Dwight's fatherly nature longed to call out caution to his son, but was held back by the manly knowledge that better he fall now than later in life.

Rema and Nancy were industriously constructing a sand castle to challenge the tide. How independent they all were, how much they enjoyed the beach, how much he loved them. The question that had surfaced in his mind earlier that day returned with a new edge. Is the life I am leading today in the city going to give these children the perspective on things I wish them to have?

A quickening of the breeze reminded him that the mountainous peninsula ten miles to the west was closing rapidly on the sun, and he set about building a fire. Like birds to a nest, they would all return to him soon unbidden, needing, just as he did, to share the splendor of sunset together. There they would huddle against a log and watch the colors dim, the boats return to Shilshole Marina, and the stars of heaven and earth wink on. They would talk of astronomy and natural history, and personal dreams would surface that somehow were never spoken of at other times. Later he would bring out the package of marshmallows hidden in his pack.

The fire established, he moved aside to escape the smoke. Marcus was working his way up the beach, alternately drawing in the sand with a stick then throwing it for Chance to fetch. The tide had almost melted the sandcastle and Rema was moving as she did when a bathroom was called for. He could see Nancy surveying the bushes for a good place. Out of the corner of his eye a flash of blackness drew him back to the camp. An old raven couple, who had skirted the picnic warily throughout the afternoon, were taking turns swooping in to scavenge for tidbits of food. Something in their cautious way made him see himself through raven eyes. He was man, very tricky, very dangerous, but also very rich, prone to leave the trail behind littered with scraps. For a moment human eye and raven eye met in mutual respect, and Dwight was moved to speak.

"Help yourself, old buddy, I won't hurt you."

The bird hopped forward tentatively, tempted by a bit of hotdog bun that lay dangerously close to the man. Dwight froze his body and slowed his breathing to encourage the quest. He could feel the raven's powerful awareness of the instant, an awareness uncluttered by civilization, an intensity that conveyed the deep joy and excitement of living. The sun, the sea, the sand, the bird, the man — all became one for a moment, partners in a cosmic dance of matter and spirit.

Then the moment passed. The crust lay beyond the limit of raven law and as the boy and the dog approached, the old bird flew off scolding the wind. Dwight knew the raven would remember the bread and probably check on it tomorrow morning, while he was on his way to the hospital. And with that thought, he smiled to himself, realizing that he no longer minded working on Saturday. Whatever he had wanted from this weekend, had wanted so badly, had happened.

• • •

At Laly Polallie Three-Eyes stopped to rest and eat. Rounding the next point would bring him in sight of

Shulshale Village, and though the mountains were about to eat the sun, he was not yet ready to return. Good berries grew here and, as was his custom, he had saved the best smoked fish for last. Besides, an hour of ebbing tide would make the river crossing easier. His travelling stopped, he urinated then searched for and found a soopalallie berry for his bad tooth. Earlier in the afternoon his mind had drifted and he had carelessly brushed against some nettles. He rubbed the stings away with salty mud. The aches in his joints and the strange new torment in his guts would not, he knew, go away so easily.

He surveyed his surroundings, deciding where to enjoy the smoked fish: out on the beach with surf and the logs and the setting sun, or up in the sheltered dunes with the birds and the summer flowers? The sight of an old gnarled snag falling off the hillside brought to mind his grandfather, with whom he had first explored this beach. His final selection kept both the snag and the sun in sight.

Many times in his forty years on Illahee strange things had washed ashore. Some had once been living things, but of strange proportions and shape. And some, like the ones at Ankutie Nauits, had been the works of men. Often these things were of great value to the tribe; boats, worked bones, baskets and shells that could not be made or found easily. Sometimes their only value was their uniqueness, objects to be traded to the foolish Tilikhum that lived across the mountains, or messages from Tahmonowis to be displayed on the walls of the longhouse. But this latest find felt somehow very different. Partly this was due to distance: extreme foreignness of materials and design. And partly this was due to closeness: the objects bore few barnacles, little seaweed and therefore had not been long adrift.

Three-Eyes knew that Illahee went on and on forever, always the same; that a hard winter would be followed by an easy one; that the salmon in the rivers moved by knowable laws through rich years and through poor; that the tribes warred amongst themselves but were in truth much the same; that joy and sorrow came in equal portions. But lately he had come to suspect that very slowly things changed. The village where he had been a boy was long ago abandoned and had returned to the earth easily. The name of that village had become only a word in the Tilikhum language for happy memories. The freshwater lake inland half a day from the village no longer froze over midwinter, and the beach beyond Dewampsh no longer had any sand. His grandfather had told him of a great white mountain in the south that had blown itself apart and of a time when little Tenas Creek was a great river.

Flashing blackness in the corner of his eye snapped him back to the present. A pair of kah-kah had spotted him chewing on fish and knew there would be droppings; perhaps, if times were plentiful, even a whole head.

Tradition said that kah-kah was the clown, wanting everything and laughing at everything. The image of him in your totem promised wit and cunning, and his black feathers brought nobility and protection. Teasing him was one of Three-Eyes' favorite pastimes. He threw the fish tail out on the beach to establish his good intentions, and it was quickly snatched up by the female and carried off. But the head he dropped tauntingly near, knowing that kah-kah would covet it, stalk it, but not dare to retrieve it that close to Three-Eyes. Thus he could entice the wily bird into a conversation. Not infrequently kah-kah spoke for Tahmonowis.

As expected, the great black bird swooped onto the beach and waddled about indecisively. Not one to mince words, Three-eyes got right to the point.

"Oh mighty spirit my people worship, what can you tell me of our beginnings and our ends?"

The bird cocked his head, almost as if he understood, and Three-Eyes saw himself reflected in the blackness, a poor man-creature who couldn't fly, who needed clothes to keep warm, who seldom had enough to eat, and who worried away his time over things about which he had no control. Then, knowing that the fish head would be there later, off flew the bird to join the female with the tail portion. He would outwait the man.

Three-Eyes stared at the last cauldron of sun trapped in a crevice of the mountains until green spots in his eyes forced him to look away. Everything spoke of endings. The end of the journey, the end of the day, the end of the fish, and his own ending soon. And the strange objects at Ankutie Nauits, an ending of . . . what? . . . a simple life? Everything except kah-kah. Kah-kah lived in the moment. That was enough.

Three-Eyes felt warm and happy inside. He knew what he could say to his people of Ankutie Nauits and for the first time in many months he sensed his true value to the Tilikhum. Tahoma he would shame for his lack of respect with a shower of many gifts, and Three-Eyes' status would rise. By returning Meetsmeets to her people, he would improve relations with the Quilcene and probably gain gifts of more value to him anyway. But most importantly he would remember and savor this moment on the beach. He would not be led astray by ankutie ghosts of ancestors or alki dreams of the future. Like kah-kah he would take care to celebrate alta . . . now. And to remind himself of this resolve he would spend the warm summer night here alone at this place and watch the stars whirl.

Tilikhum

Tilikhum. The Chinook word for people. Also relations, relatives, associates, family, folks, friends, kin, kindred band, tribe, fellow nations, population, person.

Something in the unique substructure of Pacifica allows time to flit back and forth insubstantially. Then, Now and When (Ankutie, Alta and Alki) merge harmoniously in the moments of the mind that accompany our being here. Whizzing over a freeway bridge on the way to the dentist, the jagged teeth of ancient mountains glitter and smoke in sympathy. The prick of the novocaine needle reminds one of the toll that toothache took from pioneer and Indian alike. The scrape of the tool on enamel becomes glacial ice scoring the rock beneath this office. While you wait for numbness to set in, Seattle News Radio reports on Seahawk scores and Indian fishing controversies, and the commercial is for condominiums named Illahee and Chuckanut. The picture on the wall is a seascape done at Shi Shi Beach, while the magazine they bring you tells of war in the Middle East, chicanery in Congress, an increase in cancer and a mother who beat her child to death because he was naughty in Sunday School. The inescapable reality and present tense of the drill is a relief, as outside the rain weeps your mixed feelings.

Somewhere between thirty-five thousand and sixty thousand years ago (during what is referred to as the "last" ice age, but should be called "the most recent"), when large portions of ocean water had been frozen on the continents and the resulting ocean level was much lower than it is today, a land-ice bridge existed across what is now called the Bering Sea, and for a brief time, in geological terms, Asia and North America were connected. Across this temporary bridge there migrated various bands of hardy primitive pre-Mongoloid Homo sapiens; a species of hominid that had evolved nearly a million years earlier in the more hospitable climate of Africa, and had up to that time spread over much of Europe and Asia. These first Tilikhum to reach the new world brought with them many of the skills and attributes that characterize the species called man, and would lead, many years in the future, to his ruthless domination of earth; language and fire, stone tools, spears and harpoons, cordage, netting, basketry and the domesticated dog. More important, however, to the eventual outcome of this story were some of the skills and cultural patterns they left behind; domesticated plants and animals, iron, the wheel and the plow, agriculture and stringed musical instruments. That is to say, things that had to do with staying put in temperate climates and would be but heavy baggage to explorers of arctic reaches.

Considering the distances and difficulties, in an amazingly short amount of time the descendants of these early explorers found their way to every nook and cranny of the land mass they had discovered; all across North America to the Atlantic Ocean, and down to the very tip of South America. To have accomplished this must have tested even man's genius at adaptability, for along the way they encountered every possible environment. Snowy, rainy mountains gave way to vast arid deserts. Old food sources left behind and new ones had to be discovered. At every turn on their roadless journey, new and dangerous plants, animals and natural phenomenon had to be studied, avoided or conquered and new ways of living absorbed into their culture.

Then, as it had several times throughout the Pleistocene, the climate warmed, the ice caps melted and the Bering Sea land bridge was submerged in ocean, isolating this surge of humanity from its source. While the larger populations of the Old World went on to develop what is considered civilization today, these peoples of the New World remained essentially hunter gatherers. The isolation, the enormous distances and natural barriers of this new land, the great quantity of foods and the lack of population pressure combined to make an Old World style civilization unnecessary. Why should a man submit to arbitrary laws of whimsical rulers when it was all too easy to move his family over the hill and live in peace? Indeed, it was essentially these same motivations that brought a new wave of immigrants to this continent fifty thousand years later (or five hundred years ago) and that drove people here to Pacifica a hundred and fifty years ago, and that even today drives a few independent pilgrims to the Alaskan tundra and an austere life without television or tonsillectomies. For these people the price that larger civilization exacts for its amenities is too high to pay.

I cannot imagine living thoughtfully in Seattle today without developing a deep relationship with the American Indian people that lived here before. Their languages decorate the maps and places with special levels of meaning. The earth beneath our feet soon shapes us just as it shaped them, from ways of cooking salmon to metaphysics. And as the bones of our ancestors begin to mix with theirs, we feel a tug of distant brotherhood. Yet I can think of few subjects so fraught with both emotional and factual difficulties. Living here in their space, vague impressions form in the backs of our minds that seem somehow important; and yet, like the motes that drift across one's eye occasionally, cannot be examined. Or when they are examined, disintegrate into a plethora of cold and contradictory facts that seem unable to support the feelings that brought them forth.

Their dim and distant prehistory is a smattering of isolated details from digs and suppositions: a bone here, a basket there, a petroglyph or two. Historical reports of our first contacts are so colored by the ignorance and prejudice of the beholder as to make them little more than tragic comments on our own history.

And then there is the holocaust, a story that surely forms the living prototype for many a science-fiction horror about an alien invasion of earth. A demonstration of evolutionary dogma concerning survival of the fittest — that is, the strong destroy the weak — that goes beyond reason and guilt to illuminate elements of Homo sapiens' behavior that we prefer to forget: a kind of super Auschwitz, Hiroshima, Black Death, Crusade that will never be exceeded, except perhaps by a real alien invasion, or more likely World War III.

And yet I must confess that in spite of all the guilt and loathing I feel towards this chapter of history, in spite of all the sympathy I feel towards contemporary Indian leaders who politic benefits for their people under the impossible guise of restitution, in spite of the deep spiritual bond I share with ancient Tilikhum brothers, I would not for a moment trade my Encyclopedia Britannica, my piano, my education or this time in history for a spear and a rock to fish from. To do so would be to condemn my own descendants to repeat the same mistakes again and again, to suffer the same fate, to remain tied to a karmic wheel of endless reincarnation and maya, the beastly darkness of innocence.

For there is sprinkled over all this Indian lore, not to mention contemporary Indian politics, a great deal of romantic fantasy; a renaissance of the Rousseauan noble savage myths and philosophies that entertained the 18th century. In fact, Redmen are men in every sense of the word: they warred, they took scalps, they tortured, they stole, they lied and they lived, by our standards, miserable lives. Their colorful superstitions may seem a relief after one's Judeo-Christian counterparts have worn stale, and their pantheistic spirits-of-the-earth a welcome contrast to the icy madness of materialism running amok, but they are still superstitions.

One should note, however, that all cultures, including our own, are built on a substructure of metaphysical assumptions . . . superstitions. Once rooted in our minds through language and religion, these assumptions so permeate our perceptions as to allow us to create truth. The separation of *I* from *It* that characterizes Western civilization, for all its great technological achievements, is such an assumption.

As the negative aspects of this assumption become more and more self-evident, revealing themselves as a gnawing inner dissatisfaction for the individual and as a grotesque, immoral, uncontrollable monstrosity for the civilization at large, one searches further and further for a viable alternative. Certain elements of Indian history and character begin to look strangely sophisticated; perhaps even of critical value in light of our own cultural traumas.

Further confusing, and often contradicting the nostalgic images of ancient peoples that play across one's mind, are the nations and individuals of Indian people living here today. For the most part their central core is unremarkably like any other middle class. They work hard, support themselves, partake of the benefits of civilization, and deal adequately with the problems it throws at us all and mind their own business. A tight ethnic racial group, they wisely shy away from confrontations with an obviously racist society, finding it more productive and more comfortable to remain among themselves. The reservation system makes this behavior particularly attractive. We see them most often at the fringes. The failures panhandling around liquor stores, weaving in and out of certain special taverns in Pioneer Square, sleeping it off in doorways and parks or scavenging discarded food at the Pike Street Market. Unable to negotiate the complex curves that make up their paths, they have succumbed to a genetic weakness for metabolizing alcohol. Pathetically understandable as the remnants of a culture devastated by change and prejudice, they are tolerated, indeed, even enjoyed as a colorful reminder of the good old Wild West. Should they become too numerous, troublesome or heart-breaking, they are carted off with their Caucasian counterparts in specialized garbage trucks known as detox wagons.

At the other extreme are the radicals burning brightly with a rediscovered self image. With great courage they have taken up the weapons of contemporary institutions and, bending them to their own needs and ways, found considerable success at righting the wrongs done their nations. Not the least of these achievements has been a rebirth of pride for the Indian peoples, a dangerous but necessary step on the road to enlightenment. Less attractive but equally prevalent are greed, a human foible shared equally by all sides in these controversies, and the temptation to make of Old World Man a scapegoat for all human misery. This Yankee Go Home tactic, so frequently used to unify small nations against a common enemy, and however successful it may be in the short term, is spiritually devastating. It substitutes hatred for understanding, condemning the future to endless repetitions of the past. It leads to unkindness, to brutality, to war, to death. It denies that we are all men on the earth; we all came to be here the same way. If we are to survive much longer, it will be as one mind.

I have summarized here some of the impressions and feelings that surround the Indian, in spite of the difficulties and contradictions, because it is a vital part of this thing called Seattle. This element in her history enriches us at every turning with a profound and unique past and just possibly a profound and unique future. For sometimes when I am out alone perceiving Pacifica's murmurs, and I stare too long into the abysmal darkness of our past, I think I see there the flicker of a phoenix rising. The glitter of some golden spiritual thread woven around Tilikhum campfires ages ago that will become the mainstay of the future. How like the universe to destroy that it might create, to subjugate that it might free. As with the stars that exploded to forge the elements of earth . . . of life.

There is in *Indian-ness* a rare opportunity for us to see ourselves in the light of a much different history of human searching. More and more often of late, thoughtful men of Western Civilization have turned to the Orient for guidance in navigating the hall of mirrors that is consciousness: to India with Satipatthana or mindfulness, to Japan with Zen mindlessness, to the Chinese Tao — exotic fruits from other branches of the tree of human spiritual development. Yet here we discover a branching way down near the roots of all culture, and many times removed from Orient and Occident alike. In the self-righteous greed of our early contacts we saw this only as pagan primitive savagery, and indeed, some it may have been. But does it stand the test of reason that man — the same man we are — could have spent fifty thousand years living on the earth rather successfully and not have discovered something? Is it possible that some of the cultures living on this continent had, before they were devastated, metaphysical substructures of great spiritual value?

My own experiences and reflections living in Seattle have led me to believe that this is indeed the case. Even a cursory study of only two languages, Chinook and Kwakiutl, has introduced me to some shocking cognitive processes where I find myself not only unable to translate a thought into English, but living in a subtly different universe. The ability of these languages to express any idea yet retain the original imagery that gave rise to the words themselves makes of any expression a poem, for one must choose words with great care. Much like Chinese, the limited earthy vocabularies force one to strip from one's Indo-European thoughts the many layers of historical veneer and deal directly with the bones of mental processes. Thus the intention of one's thoughts is first carefully structured and then preserved indefinitely.

Of equal importance in this linguistic process, however, is the powerful presence of Pacifica. Because of the newness of civilized man to its shores, the environment that gave rise to these languages is still largely available to experience. Somehow this environment and these languages interact to create an intellectual ambience of direct experience difficult to frame in English syntax.

In September on the warm sunny banks of some nameless mountain, far from the sight of any civilization, with only the sounds of cascades of water and Western thrush falling on your ears, the purple taste of huckleberries on your tongue and the smell of forest and snow serenading your nose, one's thoughts tend not to be abstractions. Those things over there are not trees, they are stories and symbols of life on Illahee. That old tall one with the thrush atop was a seedling with your great great great great grandfather, and will be here long after you are gone. The skinny bent one is ill and has become a home for fungus. The one in between lost all its north side branches ten years ago when the log at its feet was blown over in a storm. Calling them trees may satisfy your childhood habits, but it does not describe them very well. *Tree-ness* comes in a million forms. Calling them Douglas Fir may be phylogenically correct and useful at the mill or among botanists, but it ignores the reality of the moment. You become acutely aware that framing into language is a limiting process with a specific purpose in mind. In Chinook jargon, one might render this scene as *klone hyas huloima hyas kakawak elip ow kopa mitlite illahee alta*. Three very different tall light green elder brothers living at this spot on the earth now.

To abstract them further, separating them from the experiencing of them, would strain Chinook syntax. Not because the words or grammar are not available, but because the separation of existence and perception — being, feeling and meaning, I and It — are foreign to the nature of the language.

It may seem amazing that any people living with trees on as intimate a relationship as is possible to imagine should have no word for tree. In fact, of course, they had many, dealing with the myriad of forms in which treeness entered their lives. Perhaps the collective term was simply too unspecific to be of any use, or perhaps it is an agricultural concept. It is interesting to note that when contact with the white man made the concept of treeness a matter of daily practical concern, they intuitively borrowed the English word "stick," which I suggest reflects nicely the utilitarian lack of feeling that went with it, for it was merely as sticks that these living historical spirits were considered.

But there is more to culture than language, and whether what remains of Indian culture today is either truly viable or representative of the real things, I cannot say. It is just dimly possible that the reservation system, for all its questionable benefits, has preserved on a few remote and traditional hearths the embers of a flame that once burnt brightly, and could, if called upon, rekindle the torch of human spirituality. That this might only happen upon the demise of "Western" civilization may seem a disturbing, or if you wish, ironic possibility. But upon consideration, far less so than other more probable projections of our near future.

Civilizations come and go as their spirituality waxes and wanes. And cultures, like all living things, evolve slowly by the processes of natural selection. The organisms of

Indianness and Western Civilization have most probably cross-fertilized in a thousand backyard garden patches randomly and unnoticed. They certainly have in mine. From these hybrids may well spring a new path for humanity to explore.

In 1853 at a small village on the shores of Elliot Bay, the governor of the newly formed Washington Territory announced the white man's intention to buy from the Indians their ancestral lands. As with most of these "treaties," no specific price was negotiated. In fact, it is doubtful whether most of the Indians understood what the celebration was all about. "Boston Man" frequently observed strange holidays that had no meaning for the Tilikhum or the cycles of Illahee that framed their lives. But there can be little doubt that one man did: Old Chief Sealth, for whom the village was named, and who was asked to speak at the ceremony on behalf of the Indian peoples. His closing words reveal an understanding far beyond any of his white contemporaries, and express for me, even today, one of Seattle's primary attributes and assets:

"... At night
When the streets of your cities and villages are silent and you think them deserted, they will throng with the hosts that once filled and still love this beautiful land.
The White Man will never be alone.
Let him be just
And deal kindly with my people,
For the dead are not powerless.
Dead, did I say?
There is no death.
Only a change of worlds ..."

The Truth

The little boy watched his great-grandmother weeding in the garden. She looked funny bent over double like that, the bow of her apron perched like a bird on her rump and jiggling to the industry of her fingers. As she waddled slowly forward, one foot at a time, it flopped from side to side exploring different configurations, the loops occasionally making circles against her dress and the tails gently patting her bottom.

Now and then she would straighten up, her right hand against her back, her left hand cocked against her hip. Then slowly she would turn to glance behind and then upwards, measuring her progress by checking the clock of the sun. For just a moment the boy studied her old and wrinkled face that managed to be both stern and friendly, both confident and bemused.

She didn't look like an Indian. Her hair was white and her skin was light. But her eyes were dark as night and with all those wrinkles it was hard to tell for sure. She lived in a nice house and went to church and didn't approve of drinking at all. But on the other hand she was definitely different. She used strange words, had some strange habits and told some strange stories. He realized suddenly that one of the different things about her was her silence. Even when she heard and understood (for she was quite deaf) she did not respond like other adults. She smiled and frowned, was angry or pleased, interested or distracted, but she seldom spoke, and when she did it was important. Somehow this seemed very Indian to him.

Behind these reflections was a conversation he had overheard last week between his mother and Auntie Belle. It had something to do with Marney living with Indians, with massacres and slaves and missionaries and family history. But when he had made his presence known, the conversation had stopped abruptly and his inquiries had met a wall of adult evasion. He recognized that wall and knew enough not to persevere. It was the same "no" quality that had to do with bathroom things, with parent's bedrooms late at night, with weddings and funerals and sometimes God in general, and always with Uncle Otis. Most of these subjects didn't interest him anyway. What little he was told about them seemed much ado about nothing.

But Indians. Those very unusual people who were beautiful and wise in books but ugly and stupid in town, who had lived here on the river before we came and been driven off, yet somehow still owned it, who his grandfather called siwash and thought of as animals, but his parents spoke of with respect and concern, Indians interested him very much. He wanted to explore this new discovery, even if it met with disapproval.

His musings were interrupted as Marney, in the upright back-easing posture, beckoned him with a sweep of her bonneted head. He lined up on her row and entered the vegetable garden, cribbing some peapods to crunch as he walked.

"Lord-a-mercy, child, they'll be none left for supper," she began with Scotch Presbyterian style, but accepted his offer to share the pickings as an acceptable gesture of greeting. At close range he studied her face, searching for clues of ancestry and present intent, and delighting in the near equality of their sizes. She was a tiny woman. He had no playmates on the farm at present, and this, plus the fact that neither of them lived in the work-a-day adult world, had created a bond that bridged the gulf of age.

"It's the wheelbarrow I be a-needing from the shed. The old wooden one, if you please, the new one is too wide for the rows."

It was a family joke. The garden was her domain and four years ago, for her eightieth birthday, his father had purchased for her a new light-weight rubber-tired wheelbarrow. But firmly set in the width of her rows and fond of old things, she never used it. During the moment it took to appreciate her request, a bumblebee explored the space around them and the boy considered how best to phrase his question. You couldn't be subtle with Marney, even when she had her hearing aid on, which she did not at the moment.

"Are you an Indian?" he yelled at her, a wave of guilt sweeping through him from the nature of the question and the sudden realization his mother might hear him from the house.

"Eh?" she said, wrinkling her brow and cocking her head as if she did not understand. But he knew that she did. Some subtle shift in her eyes or her posture spoke to him of emotion. It was one of Marney's characteristic ruses to understand only what she wished. Whispers and signals behind her back about alcohol being served or illnesses she quickly pieced together. Doctors orders, however, or other inconveniences she could never seem to hear, no matter how loud or how many times they were spoken.

"The wooden wheelbarrow," she repeated, closing the subject.

His courage exhausted and his wit defeated, the boy trooped off to the tool shed to do as bidden and to assess whatever damage he had caused. Would she be cold to him? Would she tell his mother? The duplicity of the adult world pressed hard against the innocence of his curiosity, and rebellious images flashed across his mind: refusing to eat turnips, sassing back. How come it was so important for him to tell the truth . . . no matter what . . . when they could fib and digress at will? His frustration found its way into a flat rock, which he skipped angrily at the river. Kerplunk said the river, not caring one whit.

The old lady watched her great-grandson trudging away on his chore, his neck bowed, his right arm striking at the air in frustration. He was peeved, and something about that brought a small smile to her face. Like his father and grandfather, he was intelligent and sensitive, wanting to understand. Like his mother and her own family, he was stubborn and willful, not easily swayed. The combination pleased her greatly.

His question struck at the dark truth in the family past that had never been properly acknowledged. Nay, not even a truth in fact, but only a possibility, a work of the devil that had introduced into her otherwise honest and fruitful life a maze of deceptions, a ghost that had haunted her marriage, her child-bearing, even her grand children. And like some Biblical pestilence, it was about to be visited upon the fourth generation.

And time was a-wasting. She was old and the Good Lord would surely come to take her soon. When He did there would be not a body left on earth who knew the real story, except Lee, of course, but he would never tell. She had felt obligated to tell him before he married Emma, as she had told both of her daughters and their intended husbands. Lee and Emma had been very much in love at the time and he said that it did not matter. But she knew that had either of their children, Marion or Jim, been born with

Indian features, it would have mattered very much. In some ways she was not even certain of her own recollections. Her mind seemed the same as always, but it played tricks on her now and then. And there had been so much dissembling over the years that the facts had become stretched out of shape. But some force deep within her, beyond everyday right and wrong, wanted very much to tell the boy everything. And that raised a host of new difficulties. How old was the boy? Six? Seven? Not old enough to understand either the facts or the feelings they gave rise to. How babies were made; how many men — even preachers, even fine men otherwise like her son-in-law Lee — were ill disposed toward dark-sinned races, how different things were with many white men and so few Indians.

She had considered these problems many times, lying alone in her bed savoring the quiet in the house and the early morning, reading from the Bible, offering little prayers and living again through her rich past. Jesus had forgiven the whore. He had treasured the little children. He himself had been a dark-skinned Jew. Nowhere could she find the source of the many fears and prohibitions that so preoccupied churches. And nowhere could she find a clear parable for her own situation. She longed to fulfill the commandment to honor thy father. Not Jonas Caruthers, whom she loved dearly and prayed for often, who had given her mother and herself an upright Christian name and home, who had sired her sisters and Otis, who had taught her both the love of Jesus and the value of truth. No, not Papa, but her real father, unnamed and unknown.

In search of help she glanced toward heaven to find the burning noontime sun high in the sky above her, and like an Old Testament miracle an angel appeared at her side. An angel in the form of her favorite grand-daughter, the boy's mother. Practical, down-to-earth, beautiful Marion. If anyone could help her, she was the one. Marion was saying something to her, smiling and ruffling her hen feathers. From this and the position of the sun, Marney could guess that she was being called in to rest.

"Land sakes," she croaked, "time does scurry by when a body's busy."

It was several days before the right moment arrived to broach the subject. Tuesday afternoon it had been on the tip of her tongue, but Mrs. Lagasee had come a-calling. And again Wednesday morning, while peeling apples . . . but the moods had been wrong. It wasn't until Thursday night, after the boy was a-bed and the men had gone bowling in Kelso that she found herself alone with Marion, and in a humor of closeness. They were sewing, she a comforter, Marion darning socks. A pleasant, womanly, chores-together atmosphere with the warm colors of the shaded lamps bathing the room in hominess and the feeling of a change in the weather exciting the evening air.

"Marion," she said, without looking up from her work, "methinks we should tell the boy about my mother."

Such are the ways of family that small clues provide whole chapters of meaning. Marion connected together the various loose ends of this remark: the overheard conversation with Auntie Belle, the boy with his great-grandmother in the garden on Monday, the moods that had possessed them both immediately after. Mimicking Marney's off-hand style, she responded with her teeth clenched across the black thread she was knotting.

"He would love that, Marney." Then, sensing that something more was intended, she added, "What about your mother?"

While readjusting the fabric draped over her legs to better advantage, Marney said a silent wordless prayer to Jesus, God, and Jonas Caruthers. "Well, now," she said looking up for emphasis, "the terrible goings-on at Walla Walla . . . her childhood as an Indian . . . the journey west . . . how the McLaughlin's discovered her with the Kwakiutl and bought her freedom . . . how Jonas took her in and taught her white man ways . . . English, Christian ways . . ." and then she got to the meat of the stew indirectly, "how I was born at Oregon City."

Marion was silent for a while considering what she knew of this history and noting the subtle inconsistency of the last statement. There had always been something puzzling about this whole business, something unspoken that lent to it indefinable weight. Her mother made light of the subject as if it were a children's tale. And her father? Yes, it was true, he avoided the subject with clever sidesteps, much the same way he did with Papa Caruthers. She recognized suddenly that she was being instructed in this matter, that Marney was leading her toward something.

"Mama," she said, using her mother's term for Marney, the term she used when she felt she was acting as surrogate daughter, "tell me the whole story."

Those were the words that Marney's poor old deaf ears had longed to hear for nearly half a century. Tears came to her eyes and a dangerous flutter to her heart. But the irony of going now at so sweet a moment made her smile and gasp once more at the breath of life. It was a warning, though, to digress no longer.

"My child, Papa Caruthers, bless his holy soul, be not my father truly. My true father be some unknown man of the Lord's choosing who had known my mother from Indian days. Such were the heathen ways in those times, that she had lain with many a man, both white and Indian, and was already quick with child when she came to Fort Vancouver, scarcely a child herself. Jonas, whose wife and daughter had died at the massacre thirteen years earlier at Walla Walla, took it to be a sign from God, and made for her a home. There I was born but six months later. Had I been dark-skinned, a half-breed siwash, all would have been different. But seeing me fair as any Christian child, and there being few single women to choose from, Jonas let the affection he held for Meetsmeets (thus my mother called herself), grow into love. Within a year she was re-christened Anna, after his first wife, and they were married. My sisters, Little Anna and Priscilla were born of that union . . . and also . . . a wee malformed boy . . . Homer he was called . . . he died . . ."

Marion longed to hear more — details of Grandma Anna's capture and character, their life in the early days and why she had not known this long before. But Marney was spent. She slumped in the rocking chair, the sewing dropped at her side, staring into the past of the cold fireplace, breathing in widely spaced gasps.

"Come, Marney, it's time for bed," she said, helping the old lady up, holding her arm as they walked together through the kitchen and into her bedroom at the back of the house, where Marion folded down the blankets.

While Marney dressed for bed and did her evening toilet, Marion warmed a cup of milk on the stove, adding just a touch of sugar. Tucked in, in her nightie and cap, propped up with pillows, her teeth out and her hearing aid off but her glasses still on and her Bible clutched in her hand, Marney was a quaint and touching sight.

Marion realized once again how, in many ways, this woman had been more a mother to her than her real mother, Emma. Emma was cool and correct and apprehensive about appearances. She and Marney were simpler, more concerned with feelings. Emma had taught Marion to behave, but Marney had taught her to cook, to sew, to garden.

With the hearing aid gone, little could be said. Besides, Marney's mind had drifted to other, closer things; when the men would get home, tomorrow's turkey, the forthcoming visit of some cousins. Marion smiled and nodded, communicating by presence and puttering about the room, adjusting curtains and collecting laundry. When the milk was finished and it was time to leave Marney to her prayers, Marion sat on the edge of the bed for a moment, held her hand, leaned close and spoke loudly into her grandmother's ear.

"Thank you, Marney. I shall treasure tonight all my life. Tomorrow we must tell the boy together."

"Well, yes. That we must," Marney responded softly. But whether she understood or not, Marion could not be sure.

Later that night, in bed, Marion related the day's events to Earle, and in retelling the story more of its elements surfaced: how the feelings among whites and Indians must have colored early times; how, in spite of Marney's appearance, the possibility of Indian blood had clouded her future; why she was so different from her sisters; why Papa Caruthers, in contrast to his peers, had been so understanding of Indian ways and aspirations, a fact that Earle had always admired greatly; how Emma and Lee, in their concern with status, propriety and class, had carefully avoided this chapter of the family history. Considering Marion's dark hair, eyes and rich complexion, they toyed with the exciting possibility of an Indian ancestor. But what, after all, did it matter, except as a key to understanding the family better? Time, history and many generations had washed away any possibility of taint, indeed, had even made it desirable. The power and goodness of their present life, their love, their children, their home on the Cowlitz, all quite overwhelmed this distant echo.

Still later, lost in her own thoughts, a wave of sadness came over Marion as she gave up the feeling of Papa Caruthers in her bones and replaced it with . . . who? A drunken trapper? A beached sailor? A fat ugly Indian guest? The experience of such unions for a twelve-year-old girl filled her with horror and she pressed against her husband's backside for warmth. Earle chuckled softly and reached over to pat her bottom.

"I still think we should use the new wheelbarrow for her gravestone," he said, looking for a release of the mixed feelings. Outside, past the garden, the river answered . . . kerplunk.

THE ARBORETUM

To err is human. To forget — 'till pain or pleasure or providence reminds us anew of each bloody fact — is also human.

The Arboretum

It is Valentine's Day 1982 and Chance and I have just returned from a walk in the Arboretum where I went to feed the ducks and celebrate my truest loves while he chased squirrels and explored smelly secrets beyond my perception. It is a very Seattle day: warm, rainy, gray, quiet. Yet mild though it is compared with most of the earth, because of the weather few people are out. The resulting recession in handouts make the birds a most appreciative audience. Ducks, ducks, ducks, ducks, cooties, seagulls, ravens, pigeons, redwing blackbirds, robins, crows, geese overhead and all flying, floating, scrambling, scrabbling, wading, waddling, squeaking, squawking, cooing, crowding, crying, nipping, chasing, begging, bullying, bellowing — far more like men of commerce than creatures of the wild.

I cannot resist applause and greatly enjoy my brief reign as the morning's only gift giver. All the time I was there I saw only one fisherman, escaping, and two bedraggled joggers maintaining their self-respect. Blessed be the rain for giving me this quiet chance to be alone again with the earth the way it really is. To see just rocks and water, sky and light and everywhere life abounding with such miraculous inevitability as to leave me awed. To smell the poking, budding, sprouting spring coming no matter what is done in the marble halls of man. To stand under a great old hemlock waiting out a squall with all those generations of my ancestors who stood there for so long. And to remember . . . Ye Gods, I had forgotten again.

What can we say of memory, that primeval property of mind so much a part of our being that we only become aware of it when it fails? Perceiving and recalling is the cake of it all, no doubt, while all the rest of civilization is but a frosting, sweet and decorative, but insubstantial by comparison. Chance knows. In that wild spot halfway between the Winter Garden witchhazel and the Quercus grove of evergreen oaks he dashes purposefully to the base of a certain giant maple where once, three years ago, he almost caught a squirrel. At that moment memory is for him a cunning and powerful weapon. Dinner before Purina. And now and then at branchings in today's trail and other choice locations that I do not understand, he lifts his leg to mark a map by means of which he may remember the way home. A written language long before hieroglyph.

The ducks know. They turn gently toward me as I approach, a possibility only. And when the breadbag appears a few of them begin to float haphazardly in my direction. But when the arm throws and a small white pellet sails into the lake, they rush across the inlet towards me in all their various forms of travel, setting up a commotion that alerts the others hidden 'round the bend. And then they see the dog and recoil abruptly, making a peculiar squeaking noise until they have determined that he is not a swimmer. Luncheon is served.

In a slow silent way the jonquils and daffodils know, too, poking their thousands of green fingers up through the winter's leafy mulch at the waxing light, preparing for next month's celebration and reminding me gently that the truly important memories are beyond consciousness.

Suddenly the fisherman starts his outboard motor. Though it is a tiny thing it grates incongruously against the natural morning sounds. As I wait for it to decrescendo into the the distance, it occurs to me that this park is in many ways an illusion. For better or for worse, man has made the earth small. We have even made our machines of memory small; tiny ingenious rapid random access chips that store and retrieve billions of bits precisely right, forgetting not one zero. How unlike living memory are these tools.

To err is human. To forget — 'till pain or pleasure or providence reminds us anew of each bloody fact — is also human. That which we do daily is there instantly at our demand, while all that which is seldom used is iffy. The ifs are interesting to study but difficult to define. I can remember finding a pebble in the creek when I was five. I cannot recall my address in New York ten years ago. Once every three years I stub my toe on the lip of the shower floor, and though it hurts like hell I cannot help laughing at my own forgetfulness. I know every note of thousands of pieces of music, yet I dare not sit down to play one of them if I have just turned the coffee pot on high. And after twenty-five years I cannot remember the sound of my mother's voice. When I heard it recently on an old home recording, it was as foreign to me as Kubla Khan. Yet at the vaguest hint of Ponds cold cream I am in her arms again.

Because I come to the Arboretum often, it is full of these kinds of memories. There off Fosters Island I tipped over a canoe and was rescued by a boatload of nuns. There in that pond with the waterfall Chance cut his front paw on a broken Olympia beer bottle. In the summerhouse up on the hill Nancy and I carved our initials with a plus between them. And under this hemlock, where I am right now, I realized that I was truly in love.

Yet sweet as these personal touches are, they are here merely because this is one of my places. They are not the reason I come here. That has to do far more with things that were here long before I came to be. Things that I pray, sometimes hopelessly, will be here long after I am gone. A place to go where one can consider civilization against the only backdrop that gives it meaning — the earth from whence it sprung. The mother that smells not of cold cream but of rotting leaves, and the father hiding there above the clouds that drives this living machine.

When I was younger I used to have to go on dangerous explorations to establish this rapport; the North Cascades, the Olympic Beaches, the Grand Canyon, the Himalayas, peak scaling and wilderness treks to test my manly mettle. Youth is a season of extremes. And no doubt the feelings and knowledge, the memories of these journeys enrich my simple stroll in a park. Were it not so habit-hidden I know that I should find the same things in my own yard. The cherry tree, the blackberries, the bird feeder. And I know that the day may come when I must read these things from a flower brought to my bedside. But for now I find them when the dog takes me out for a walk.

It is a ritual, of course, like Christmas or Ramadan, weddings and funerals, national holidays and astronomical events. Celebrations we use to help us remember what life is all about. A gentle but shocking reminder that we are a tiny almost meaningless speck slipping inexorably toward our personal end about which *it* cares nothing. And suddenly the joys and sorrows of our day-to-day life vanish in meditation; a brief moment of mindfulness where *now* becomes everything, where, uncluttered briefly by the physical demands of staying alive materially, and unconfused by the illusions of expectation or regret, simply being is enough. So powerful is this medicine of the spirit that even one flashing glimpse of the cosmos in all its glory is enough to alter a man's life forever, enough to sustain him through many a cabin-bound winter of the soul, to give him courage and good-heartedness to share with all creatures.

And then, thump! Chance drops a stick at my feet begging me to play some game that he can share. And full of the joy that comes only from the love of everything, I take up the challenge and play stick with him for real. Not as a man would, but growling, barking, lunging and leaping, running, sneaking, hiding, finding and pretending canine cunning that I find within me somewhere deeply stored, memories of my mammal ancestors somehow with me still. And more. Turned backwards on my path I seem to sense behind the mist of this man, me, today, all the incarnations that have brought my seed to be. I am a small furry creature hiding in the dark. I am a slithering mud-lover guarding my eggs. I am back in the sea again swimming toward the light. From here it is clear that all creation is my family tree.

All of this while Chance is licking his paw and gnashing his teeth at a flea. For in reflection, like dreams, the arrow of time is bent into a circle. Eons pass in instants and I can see that by some mental mirror looking back has much to do with looking ahead, that memory is also our instrument for projection. Because I have been here before, *déja vu*, I can, for the most part, see the year ahead. It will be like this. . .

Soon the invisible sun will drop behind Capitol Hill and, recharged, it will be time to go home. To shop and cook a meal and do the dishes and share with those I love my cosmic luck. To urge them into better things by being better things myself. To befriend, to be kind to, to counsel, to listen, to work, to grapple with, to laugh and to wait.

Soon the promised spring will arrive, always the same yet always more beautiful than remembered. The daffodils and jonquils will bloom and the cherry. The maples and chestnuts will cover stark winter views with new green green. The ducks will pair off and disappear, returning with ducklings following, but indolent and particular from overfeeding and parental caution. The sun will come out and Azalea Way will explode into a vulgar spectacle of blossoms that makes the *Sunday Times* center section, and will be, for a few weeks, *the* place to be in Seattle. Crowds of happy humans released at last from their wintry dens will stroll through the splendor, oohing and aahing and tying their unused parkas around their waists, mouthing the virtues of the Pacific Northwest. The very young will romp, getting their feet wet and grass stains on their knees. The young will Frisbee and admire one another's curves and bulges so long hidden. The not quite young will plan their gardens, house repairs and vacations. The old will arrive on busses for the annual plant sale, discussing the fine points of primroses and missing the blue spruce at the top of the hill that October took forever.

Soon the Nature Walk will be clogged with types — runners, swimmers, fishermen, photographers, people pushing bicycles, people pulling children, dogs pulling people, people watching people watching. There will be new graffiti in the freeway underpass, while on the Acropolis of unused highway ramps the daring divers will entertain. The nude gay beach will simmer with suggestive glances and in the cooler groves and alcoves touchers will touch and clutchers clutch. Yet only the old gold carp in the Tea Garden pond will languorously mate for real.

Blossoms will fall and pods form and tassels dangle and cotton blow and bugs buzz and crawl and work and nests form and sprinklers hiss and people tan and play and tire as long light days drive each thing to its limit. It will be the season of too much.

Too much for Chance and I, at least (except for the occasional out-of-town guest to tour), during this carnival season when sunlight and society are searching out all the dark and secret places, when walks in the woods become promenades in the park, when there is no private place to take a leak and all our thoughts must remain on the leash of good behavior. During these times we will stay away. We will clutter up our yard with tables and chairs and blankets and coffee cups and beer bottles and gnaw on hibachi hamburgers and old bones with summer-evening friends and neighbors. Late at night, when Animal Patrol has been tucked in and said its prayers, we will explore the circle of the moon skating on the circle of Green Lake, or stroll randomly through the many quiet empty streets of houses, stirring up watchdogs here and there, chasing a careless cat into a tree, discovering a quaint little cottage tucked away that we never knew was there and forming in our mind fictional families to fit each house's hints.

This will be the time to take longer trips back to the wilder worlds that surround us. West to the wet and watery places, east to the dry and open spaces and up to the rocks and snow and beginning of things. We will revisit childhood and youth, reflecting long and hard on all that has changed, and savoring those few things that have remained. It will be the time to go, to get away, to rattle our ruts, change our courses and worry our habits. To learn again by leaving why we love our home so well.

It will not be fun. My legs will get scraped by the brush and I will get stung by a bee. Chance will get cheatgrass between his toes and porcupine quills in his nose. Our feet will be sore and we will tire of fast foods, highways, gas stations, strange smelling beds and unknowns. But we will do it, and we will do it again. For we are making space in our heads, space that will, in the long winter ahead, be filled.

Perhaps it is just the old habit of schooldays, but when September comes the yellowing leaves and the crisper air seem to say enough of this foolishness, it is time to work. Time to ready the house for winter and store up nuts. There will be projects to begin and projects to complete. There will be plays and concerts to attend. Contracts and committee meetings and paper drives for the school and choir rehearsals and car repairs and plants to repot and anniversary parties and bills to pay and letters to write and dentist appointments and rabies shots and an endless list of activities that make civilization what it is today — physically amazing but spiritually confusing.

The Arboretum, as if to comment on this madness, will turn suddenly a thousand shades of fall and will be briefly once again *de rigueur* for weekend strolling. Oooh, ahhh, look at that one!

But there will be little time to look as the days grow short again and the parade of ancient holidays drives our frantic tempo faster still. Halloween, where for one day only we cast off our costumes and appear as what we really are: ghosts and skeletons, unrecognized kings and queens, masked men making merry. Thanksgiving, where only too much is enough, where we can see at last that we will live through the coming winter. And finally the solstice, the rebirth of the sun, the end and the beginning. By New Years I will be numb and dazed by a surfeit of too much of everything. All the hectic affirmations will have left me out of balance and, like a sleepy child needing a nap but not wanting to miss anything, I will fuss unreasonably at the needed and necessary negation of winter. The damp gray inhospitable weather will lock my doors and close my shutters, and for six weeks I will stare at the walls brooding about nothing or pace nervously about the house muttering meaningless whys.

Then it will be that the facts and figures of the world of men will press upon me painfully. My thoughts will dwell on the politics of corporate greed versus social need, on the demons of racial hatred and religious fanaticism, on the impossible choice between freedom and survival. Suddenly it will seem trivial whether most of us go by holocaust or starvation, and I will toy with selfishness as a sound policy of enlightened self-interest. The escapes usually available to me, sports, the media, the arts and sciences, all will turn against me, mocking my morality, and make caring at all seem foolish and unsophisticated. With horror I will see at last that, despite all the achievements of individual men, the *Bach Preludes*, the Taj Mahal, the very mosaic of knowledge itself, despite all these things man, collectively, is not a rational animal.

Chance, of course, will not see it this way at all. For him it will be a simple matter of boredom and lack of exercise. He will nag and pout, and he will punish, disobeying on purpose or biting my shoe too hard until finally his dogly wisdom will break through my humanly funk, and I will realize that, rain be damned, it is time to go out for a walk.

And thus it is that I will find myself standing under this tree in the Arboretum, pulling it all back together, and remembering.

Ye Gods, I had forgotten again.

NINE POEMS

Hubbard Miller

Climbing

For my brother, Jolly

Out away from the rage of the city
after the last farmhouse and fence
upon a road ever rougher
upon a path ever dimmer

up through the warm fertile valleys
up through the dark whispering forests
up through the spring in September meadows
up up up again up

back through the trails of old men's stories
back past the dawn of upright walking
back past the line twixt plant and beast
past the barest brown lichen life

and out again out, free of design
onto the fields of rocks and ice
sun and stars, wind and spirit
whence it all began

1981, Hannigan Pass

Apis

I am watching a species of bee
examine my tennis shoe rim

He's a high-country species that I haven't seen
the tennis shoe's all news to him

I know that his program cannot include shoes
I wonder if mine, should I ask

Or what will I do if I come to a shoe
that is equally far from my grasp?

I watched him to see what the answers would be
but I watched him too closely I found

For just then he thought of a queen he'd forsaken
and off flew the bee with this species untaken

In case you are wondering make no mistaken
the tennis shoe stayed on the ground.

1976, Gothic Basin

Hubbard Miller

Me

So I found myself
  scared shitless
    clinging
      to the side
        of a mountain
    digging
      in the pocket
        of my shorts
    trying
      desperately
        to find
    a certain
      special
        pencil.

1977, Chair Peak

Walking On Logs

Walking on logs
is like
playing with fire
before it is started
is like
four dimensional dancing
in English
is like
testing the edge
of a very sharp knife

Walking on logs
is like
fun
at work
is like
playing a game
in which you are the ball
is like
falling
. . . . . . almost

Walking on logs
is like
planning ahead
times ten
is like
spinning a web
on a skeleton
is like
history
repeating itself

Hubbard Miller

Walking on logs
is always special
walking on wet logs
walking on little logs
that tip
that roll
that might.
walking on big logs
far off the ground
over rock
over water
over logs

Walking on logs
is like
continued stories

I was a hemlock
a great tree
three winters ago
a storm got me
I was beached here
last full moon
perhaps I will rest now

I was a fir
I was felled to make houses
but I broke loose
and returned to my friends

Walking on logs
   is not like
            walking on anything else
   it is not like
            walking on logs is easy
   it is not
            walking on logs is hard
walking on logs is not for everybody

Walking on the graves of ancestors
in front of the children

1978 Teawhit Head

Hubbard Miller

Mate

I urge, I lead, I beg, I sweat, I drive;
with love I fight to get you up the mountain.

And yes, I lie: we're halfway now (we're not)
just up above, ahead, around the bend.

You try, you smile, you brave the crossing logs
the muddy bogs, the scratchy brush, the bugs.

By burning midday sun this romance cools;
to reach the top I must go on alone.

• • •

Oh my sweet darling waiting there below
I see you now, one very special speck;

If only you could be here once to know
what love it was that forced you on this trek;

And why I come back here from time to time
to climb the images that will be rhyme;

And while I'm here to offer up a prayer
of thanks that I am here and you are there.

4 July 1981, Snoqualmie Peak

Little Hurts

We've taken the kids for a hike in the woods
to play with the toys that are real;
to romp and scramble and drink from a stream
and escape the cage of the wheel

But it's hard for me to remember
this is not an ascent of K-2;
that it's only a mile back to the car
and that less than the best will do.

So what if they get their feet all wet
or drop their food in the dirt;
who teaches better, NO and DON'T
or cold and hungry and hurt?

Their new little bodies repair well now
from a bump or a scrape on the knee;
some day when they finally try for the top
they'll remember and step carefully.

But still I NO and DON'T and bitch
about drying boots too near the fire;
and warn about nettles and green covered rocks
and refuse them the chance to climb higher.

They'll come here some day when I'm not around
and scramble up till they have dared
to meet the terror of truth on the rocks
and know what it is to be scared.

Then slowly, with eyes in their testing toes,
they'll inch back down. Prepared
by the NOs and DON'Ts and courage that comes
with the long ago love that we shared.

July 1981, Raging River

Logjam

Iron water greenish red
Gray logs living dead
a surface scratched by skeeters skating in between

it mirrors magic mountains rising
cloud shapes merging white snow melting
water there at once in all its forms to ponder

and down beneath the ooze and awful
polliwogs long turned to frogs
a microworld where time has slowed past telling

where once again the primal stew
can mix and match all things anew
and there by chance begin another me or you

Great Spirit grant that I in dying
can lay out my bones for frying
in the sun as have these sacred trees

to let the bugs and mosses eat me
back into some form more fitting
than the form of this man sitting making words

28 June 1981, Red Mountain Trail

Hubbard Miller

6000 Seconds of Silence

Forgive me cosmos chaos,
But I am pissed.
You shot John Lennon.

Oh, I can see you now, hiding in your office,
Shuffling papers, looking for a clause that excludes you;
Pointing your finger at other universes, asking,
Lord, is it I?

And you, America, is it you?

You latter-day cowboys in fancy chrome pick-ups
Who rod around Saturdays shooting up road signs and
Killing off coyotes to prove you have penises.

You did it.

You righteous Republicans safe in the enclaves of
Power insured by the system it serves:
Writing up reasons why you should be rulers and
Tsking your tongue at the poor.

You did it.

You mesmerized hippies, dancing your disco,
Popping your poppers, doing your dope;
Living off daddy 'cause rock & roll records cost money
But work is a bummer.
Strong enough to march for peace
But not to fight for freedom.

You did it.

And all of you bland, born-again bigots, afraid of science,
Afraid of sex, ready to sacrifice all thought
To force the world to its knees
In your church.

You did it.

And you, Black brothers, so honky and hip,
All hung up on your racist trip.
Whenever life takes a heavy turn
You blame it on whitey and burn, baby, burn.
Why don't *you* invent some miracle cures?
Was John's soul really that different from yours?

Respect yourself. Respect other men.

And, oh, damn, I did it, too.

So lost in my land of music and friends;
Above the storm of political ends.
Understanding was all I needed to do
And thus, and thus, I did it too.

Why? Because there are too many of us
And we must rape the earth to live.

But I understood.

Why? Because in the struggle between freedom and security,
Freedom must lose.

But I understood.

Why guns are important to macho studs
Why Gods are important to flocks of sheep
Why drugs are important to groupie youths
Why laws are used by guardians of hordes.
Why all the various fantasy trips cannot give way
To the beautiful truth:

That we could live together in peace.

But forgive me cosmos chaos
I cannot understand why you shot John Lennon.

Six Thousand Seconds of Silence.

Hubbard Miller

Independence Day

Across this silent canvas of the dawn
In loving lines of liquid fire are drawn
The stars and stripes of freedom from the dark.
"I love the Earth," proclaims the Meadowlark.

She sings again as father Sun's first rays
Now move the Earth to answer such sweet praise,
And breathing life upon the Aspen choir
A grove of sparklers spew forth silver fire.

Awake! Awake! Now hear the barnyard news
Red Rooster trumpets cock-a-doodle-doos
That burst like rockets on the morning air
And leave a mist of milkweed drifting there.

Down in the swale where the quail quivers,
Where greenness marks imaginary rivers
Amid whose murmuring there glows
The burning embers of the wild Rose.

While high above it all our banner flies
Great Eagle lord and master of the skies,
Who warns the morning with his cruel cries
That life through death shall come as no surprise.

4 July 1980, Rendezvous Road
Winthrop, Washington

SEVEN LETTERS

[These are the only letters from Hub that I saved. Our paths diverged in the 60s. I went to Spokane, then Seattle, then Los Angeles, then Johnston Island, then L.A., then Los Altos, then Saigon, then L.A., then San Diego, then Palo Alto, then Selah, Washington, then San Diego. When I was in Selah, I took my son, Wyatt, and we went to Seattle to visit Jolly and Hub. Then Hub and I started to write back and forth.—wls]

16 March 81

Dear Spencer:

A quick note before it all hits the fan. Which reminds me of death; isn't it wonderful . . . it will all be over. No check book to balance, no enigmas to meditate away. Furthermore, thinking about it makes me relish things like doing the dishes, slugs, having the car serviced and all the other chores of today that interfere with the real work, which is, of course, thinking about death.

Why don't you send me your current output. I promise I will tell you its good no matter what I think!

(Phone call from Opera about per diem.)

I am currently performing the show I wrote for the Cultural Enrichment Program in the schools. When I look out over that sea of little faces sometimes I think about all the bliss that created them. It is a good show and most of the kids enjoy it.

Along with your letter I was offered a chance to buy retirement property in Arizona; a real western vacation on farms and ranches . . . distributed from New York, and a list of discounts from Radio Shack.

I enjoyed our evening very much also; we have always been friends whether we like it or not. Who else can remember "turn left on Maple" when the damned blinker was already flashing! [Hub is referring to my father's most annoying backseat driver mannerism. — wls]

(dog in garbage can. Chance demands retribution.)

(coffee boils over)

I haven't been writing much in the last few weeks. Somehow performing and creating conflict. When I am not creating something I get frustrated, pensive, a little crazy. Part workaholic withdrawal, part sense of loss. During those periods I do the busy work, copying parts, making tapes, and cleaning up the yard for spring.

I think I had better bring this to an end; singer arriving soon to work with me.

Lost
In a mind I call Me
I found a place I call
You

But
Holding my breath I tiptoed away
Lest I disturb a thing I call
Us

Hub.

PS. I need to meet the rest of your family.

21 May 1981

Dear Bill:

Sorry I haven't been able to write recently. One thing and another. I was on tour for a week performing my show (WATCH OUT!) in the schools. We did the Olympic Peninsula from Neah Bay to Port Townsend. Then I got a horrendous cold which laid me back for two weeks. That plus the everyday peedle-wheedle. I dropped you a post card but I don't recall mailing it.

I am hard at work writing the music for *Antigone*, to fulfill my Seattle Arts Commission grant. I am scoring it for all the bass instruments; double-bass, contra-bassoon, tuba, piano (playing on the strings only) and percussion. It will be "interesting" if nothing else. Sunday they premier my woodwind work *Other Blues* at the Art Museum. In two weeks a small company is doing an old work of mine, *Pied Piper*, in the Opera House (ballet). A singer is doing five of my songs on his recital in three weeks, and a pianist is playing a twenty-minute piece of mine that I just finished, *Cherry Tree*. So you can see I'm up to my ears in my own output.

In case you didn't get the card from Neah Bay, I repeat, I loved your poem. As you can sense from the mundane level of this letter I am not feeling very creative this morning. I just returned from the dentist which doesn't help. But I wanted to drop you a note anyway. I am glad, for you, that you got your house sold. I wouldn't move to California for all the bat crap in Carlsbad, even though I know Nirvana can be achieved anywhere if one looks inward, and remains deeply committed to NOW, at this moment here, immediately!

I do not long for my childhood or even a womb to rent or buy. Partly because it is always with me anyway, and partly because I am very happy right here. But I do wish that my bones didn't ache at night; and I would gladly give up my reduced insurance rates for some smoked silvers.

Hubby

4 Jan '82

Dear Bill:

Ye Gods and Purple Horsefeathers! Just to type '82 is enough to rattle my dry old aching bones a bit. There you are in the rain reaching out; and here I am in the snow, responding. Once more a mutual winter of discontent. You speak to me of your questions, quandaries, quagmires, wondering wanderings, mists and mysteries, missions and miscalculations, funks of all colors, and perhaps even rages. Ah yes, ain't it the truth; I do know what you feel. I, too, am plagued by idiot demons mouthing solipsisms like, "If you're so smart why aren't you rich?" And while I long ago accepted being poor as the price I must pay for being free, the day-to-day pressure of bills unpaid and the expectation of old age with not a single asset weigh heavily upon me.

Treacherous also are the icy doldrums; periods when, even given the time and space to create, I cannot produce anything worth the paper it is written on. Sketches in my notebooks that seemed so pregnant at the time reappear as redundant drivel. And there taunting me, as I cross to the kitchen for more coffee, is a trunk full of projects representing years of effort that will most probably never be heard. It will collect dust in some family attic until I am long forgotten and then be recycled to the earth from where it sprung.

The phone rings and I am offered employment. For $500 and two months of work I can do a band arrangement of "Ah Sweet Mystery of Life" and "Sweetheart." Or the Arts Commission is giving grants for Composer in Residence at a ghetto elementary school. No Thank You.

And what of those who have managed to tap the springs of commercial success; God knows the book and record stores are brimming with newly published "things." How extremely well they demonstrate the age they represent. An enormous amount of facts, figures, photographs, reproductions of things past; truckloads of trash, fads, gimmicks, promotions and tricky amusements for the groundlings to buy, some of it briefly entertaining; a few fine films, novels, poems or paintings, technically superb and eminently justified, but offering little new in terms of philosophical or artistic achievement, almost as if everything worth saying has been said. Very occasionally one comes across a small and simple thing, a song, a poem, a watercolor of such profound beauty that briefly the light of consciousness burns, and one is moved to care again. But for the most part the sheer massive volume of the material displayed overwhelms any impression left by a single item. The whole is profoundly removed from the sum of its parts by a Malthusian quantum leap into seeing yourself as a fraction far smaller than you had yet imagined.

Etched diabolically on the other side of this coin is the all-too-human need to make (facio), to do, to act upon, to create; a byproduct no doubt of the mammalian learning mode of play. To shuffle and reshuffle and reshuffle again that bone in our mouth randomly searching for some new angle to get at the meat. Not enough for us merely to reproduce ourselves materially; the body does that for us all too well. But in the mind, by that attribute which we for so long called God's Image, we do play with things until they form anew, and these are our true children. Living on in the mind of Man as long as man shall be, and evolving as do all things.

And suddenly, we are middle-aged, acutely aware that the deadline approaches. Too old and wise to believe any longer that man is a rational animal, and will thus escape the doom he has built for himself. For them the patterns of greed and suspicion, race and religion, Kulture and creed, country and king are too deeply set to forego; besides, has not science brought us all this evil; there are some things man was not meant to know. Yet we are too old and wise to accept any of these fantasy illusions as our own escapist balm. For us it is obvious that ultimate truth is not possible; yet that does not make lying one whit easier.

In spite of all this academic rambling, carefully thought out through much hard work and luck, I am at heart a primitive. All this weighs too heavily upon me only when I think too much as they do. If I ask myself, "Are you published?" "Are you rich?" I fail miserably. But if I ask myself, "Was not that last piece I wrote beautiful; is it not in fact as fine as anything you have ever heard?" and the answer is yes, which it often, but not always, is, then I feel differently. I am, after all, the ultimate judge of my universe, and it is my own critical self that I must please first and foremost.

If I dwell too much within the petty circle of today things look gray and hazy; the Russians, the Arabs, the Republicans and the damn publishing industry. Yet if I take even one step back, to the earth which made me, already I am free and happy. The wind and the water, the plants and animals, the mountains, the sea and the stars, all become my brothers. The privilege of living when I did, at what must be the peak of this civilization, with enough freedom from want and enough freedom of information to come to see, through science and art the oneness of it all, as no king or poet, whomever he might be, has ever known before, this I treasure. This consciousness that lives in my mind is made up of everything that ever happened; the big bang beginning and the birth and death of stars that forged the elements now aching in my bones; the little watery speck of Earth that quite accidentally met the conditions necessary for molecular biology; the vast evolutionary families around me that are but roads I did not take; and there, the road I did take with my dog, Chance, of mammalian play and love; the curious primate corner with hands and tools; and man himself with fire and speech and knowledge passed on past death. And all those men who lived before me, some like Socrates and Shakespeare, who sent me messages of what they came to see, and many more unknown slaves, yet equally important, who lived and died in misery building temples of capital that a few lucky others like myself might have leisure enough to reflect.

If all this seems romantic nonsense to practical men then let it be so; it pays me far more dividends than any stocks and bonds. For I am happy and I am not afraid to die. I am acutely aware of every instant as life passes through me; last night's carrot transformed into this paragraph; and that poor dumb chicken that I just put in the oven will, through the lens of my consciousness, read Scientific American from cover to cover.

It is 24 degrees out and all of Western Washington is covered with at least four inches of whiteness. I find it a delightful contrast and a welcome reminder of how mild it is here. However, as usual, it has become a media event, with exaggerated trauma on television far surpassing the real thing. People creep home to watch it on TV; only then is it real. Dwight is fighting his way home via a grossly overcrowded Metro (he couldn't even get here last night), and Chance is in the front yard gnawing on a gigantic bone provided by one of the neighbors. Jolly and Dori are still in Winthrop unable to return due to weather. Lee and Teresa are in Mexico for the month. You are in San Diego, Mother and Dad are gone and that is about it.

Love,

[drawing of a cube]

Cube (type 1A non-Rubric)

[Undated, no salutation. I'd sent Hub a story, called "Bliss" that I was working on. I tossed it out years ago.]

Picture if you will Hub's kitchen in Seattle. The typewriter is set on the table such that, when staring out the window past the bird feeder, and through the Cascade Mountains, like a beam of neutrinos he searches out Selah. Having never been there the images that form in his mind oscillate irregularly between pastoral and drab. All of them are real. None of them are real. Just as the Hub that forms in your mind as you read this is, and is not. Just as the Hub that forms in my mind is, and is not. You are one thing; your picture of yourself is, by the nature of consciousness, another; Hub's picture of your picture of you is again another. The neutrinos scatter for a second as again another picture is formed. All of them are real, and none of them are real.

When writing in the first person, it is a funhouse of mirrors. The author and the "I" are close to the same only in the most autobiographical possible presentations; and then only when it is done with enough depth and length to allow the reader to piece together those things which even the author has not realized. In the short story the I must, of necessity, be extremely limited. The reader does not care or need to know of the real you; only the you as it relates to the story. Thus, page 25 leaps out at one as a sudden shift into a personal reality, and not part of this story. The high point of a finale must come very close to the end. Either the final words are a cameo poem that capture the whole experience, or they must suddenly suggest a new way of considering what has happened.

I like Bliss a lot. It has moral meat, and it is seasoned with real experience. That is where we always do our best work; when we are writing about something we truly know. Mountains I know intimately; like old friends, my ancestors. But they are the Cascades, the Olympics and the Wallowas. I could not write about the Carpathians, Pyrenees or the Andes. (I'm not even sure I can spell them [he couldn't].) In the truest sense all writing is autobiographical, because you have to have lived it to write well about it. But still the God Damned "I" is a problem. Especially when "you," that is, the real you, are the one who made the correct moral decision. The comments you made in your letter point out that you sense the problem. I hope my dwelling on it isn't boring.

Two more short comments jotted in the margin while reading.

Straightforward descriptions of people or background must either be critically important to the meaning of the story, or must be relayed with some artistic pyrotechnics. For the most part they tend to sound like college writing courses if not so handled. Take, for example the description of Jill arriving at lunch. Jill's attractiveness is more than demonstrated by Bliss's reaction. I don't need to have it shoved down my throat. I feel the same way about the Peninsula weather report. The sunshine and air will seep into an outside lunch anyway.

The second and last comment is a vague one to be sure. I sense a certain lack of, or resistance to, musicality; that is, poetic awareness of the sound of words, the return of themes.I would read your writing aloud and change a word here or there to add rhyme, alliteration and metrical interest. [He then gave a couple of examples, which no longer matter.]

Finally (I have got to go to work on my own things) the piece is obviously a catharsis and I am delighted to see it. Like Mt. St. Helens the true BS is emerging and I know it feels good. It matters little now whether you are in Selah, Sausalito or San Diego. All places are the center of the universe, and the people who perceive it or misperceive it are everywhere. You have to manipulate them sometimes to get them to pay you, that's the American Way. But the most important thing is to put it on paper the way it really is to you.

Hube.

[Handwritten.]

3 Mar 82
Chehalis, WA.

Bill:

For the last three weeks, and the following two, I am touring Washington doing elementary school performances of my epic show: *WATCH OUT! Or the music will get you.* Paid for by the State Arts Commission under the line-item heading "cultural enrichment," it is really more "cultural exchange" as few children would be foolish enough to trade the clean, open, healthy countryside for the questionable pleasures of urban blight, including symphony-opera-ballet-theater-et. al. Still, it is a good show, they love it, and I make $200/day. As you see, though, it has kept me away from the typis writeris. Perhaps if you shove this up your word processor it will become intelligible.

Act Theatre will open a showcase of Seattle songwriters called *5 x 5* of which I am ⅕ on Mar 13. Then on Mar 29th I will give a reading of a new theater piece of mine called *Dandelions* for an invited audience. I hope to get a production as it is very good. All this to explain I am very busy.

I like the beginning of your story. Let me see the end, too. (I can be mercilessly demanding because when I have works simmering too I exist in that no-mans'-land between real life and my perking fantasy that becomes painful).

Because I am fatigued from heavy performances in Pe Ell and Adna, I will have to keep this short. Enclosed excerpt from my diary for you to flush. Family & friends all fine here. Dori doing Fiddler on Roof. Say hello to M. Mouse.

Love,

Hube

Hubbard Miller

I am addicted
  to music
    cigarettes
      and thinking . . .

I cannot live
  happily together
    without them

Although I see
  the folly in
    it all

And even envy
  sometimes
    those many many

Who are free
  like Buddha
    to come and go
      unhooked

I cannot help
  at last
    being thankful
      it is so

For, were it not
  no matter what
    achievements I might claim

Even if
  the many golden threads of metaphysics
    I could weave together into sense

And answer, finally,
  that last pre-cadential
    why?

Still, this one thing
  I would not savvy really:
    Addiction.

Seven Letters

Begun 3 Apr 82
Completed 19 Apr

Dear Willie:

Sorry I haven't written more lately; I have been very busy with production. (Not creation mind you, but production.) I was on tour all March doing school concerts. Then I had the A.C.T. show (flyer enclosed) to get going. Then I did a full evening concert of my songs with Dori and two other singers. It has all been very successful, artistically, but economically niggardly. My mailbox is filled with touching little cards, deliveries of flowers and balloons from admirers who wish me to know how much they enjoy my music. It is also filled with bills I cannot pay, income tax forms I must deceive and the usual quantities of junk mail soliciting retirement property or IRA accounts. The late spring weather has been equally mixed and confusing; snowing in the early morning to snarl commuters and set a tone of survival, and then, chameleon-like, transforming itself into a balmy afternoon with blossoms blowing and lovers strolling.

And all this set against a background murmur of the world going to hell in a handbag. Hatred, fear, greed, cruelty, stupidity and worst of all, the thoughtless momentum of past half-truths grinding on out of control. An equation in which, no matter how much brilliance or insight we find to factor out the quantities of one side, the other side remains quite simply . . . Too Many People.

Over the last two years I find myself more and more sitting down to the typewriter rather than the piano to express myself. Partly this is because the production of music is so incredibly time consuming and expensive. And partly it is because many of the things I wish to communicate are better said in words. Just as I know I have a talent for music and am naturally good at it, I know that I do not have that same natural talent for words. But I have lived a rich and interesting life, I do know how to work hard and somehow I must anyway.

This tack in my life began with poetry. I spent several months last summer collecting together from notebooks, diaries, wrinkled pieces of paper, hiking maps and memory, to see what it looked like when assembled. I completed, polished, typed and retyped, turned a few into songs, and even sent a few of them to publishers. I got nice letters back. Then I began a collection of stories about my childhood and had these Xeroxed for Xmas presents The response from my friends was very gratifying. At present I am at work on several short journalism pieces (essays, stories, actually just reflections) about living here in Seattle today.

I have no illusions about being a successful writer, for even though I know there is an audience out there, just as with music I can only reach it through publishing, and that is a world I cannot deal with. But I also know that I need a vicious but understanding editor before these things are truly "done."

In the past I have not sent you my "word" things because . . . partly because that is your bailiwick, partly because our styles are so vastly different that I feel certain that many of them will annoy you — I am so romantic — and partly because I think, in some small way, I fear your comments. But, it has reached a point where, in order to communicate to you what I am up to lately, it is easier to send Xeroxed material than rewrite it all in the form of a letter. It is, after all, the ideas that count, not the art form or the style. At least then I will be free to go on working knowing that I have written Bill a long overdue letter.

Love,

Hub.

P.S. Jolly, Dori, Lee, Teresa, Vincent and Jason all fine, if a bit caught up in it all.

P.P.S. My regards to Southern California.

Two-niner September

Willie:

Sorry I have not responded to your new life sooner; between moments of enlightenment and trying to make ends meet there is but little time. It sounds like you are well situated and that is pleasing. I hope it spiritualizes into something that leaves you enough time to write your own stuff also; partly because I like what you write, and partly because, if you can't, you won't be happy.

I did quite a bit of writing during the hot weeks of July and August. Dwight and I took a nostalgic trip to Wallowa County and I wrote a piece for the Chieftain. [This is "Journey Home" in The Double Key section.] When the mailbox began to fill up with letters from old-timers who had dug what I had to say, I knew it had been published. Even the crabby old motel manager who did not want to rent to "hippy with dog" was moved. I also collected a few poems which I have numerous rejection letters now collecting. I will enclose them as, knowing the business, you might have some suggestions as to what to do with them . . . not that please.

But as the fall rains returned I moved back into music. I am putting together an evening's entertainment for three singers and myself. Wherever I perform my songs I get standing ovations and numerous requests for the music. I am going to try to publish them, and will use this show as a vehicle for their development. I have fifty more school performances coming up this year through the State Arts Commission. I have two dance therapy workshops to play, one in S.F. one in Louisville, a children's theater piece to write for a group in Missoula. That brings my projected income for the next year to $11,500.

Then I have a possibility of doing a commercial piece for Boeing's 767 due to roll out January 13th. If it materializes it will involve an orchestra piece to be performed by the symphony, a trip to Rio de Janeiro to get the ideas of some Brazilian bigshot, and another $5,000. We all know what that kind of project is like; a PR burger smothered in bullshit. But I have always wanted to go to Rio.

However, I have not had a cent of income for July, August and September and I am without rent money. As a good friend of mine says, "If something doesn't happen pretty soon, something's going to happen." In light of that thought I must close off this newsy but uninspired report and get my ass in gear. I repeat that I am glad to hear you are housed and employed. I will write something more memorable when the fancy strikes me.

Love,

Hubbo

Little Stream

I

Little stream upon the mountain side
Water spirit be my guide
Teach me how to laugh and play
Let me learn from you to flow
Longing to return to Mother Sea
You're just like me
Making up a song as you go
Oh take me back
Take me back
My friend.

II

Little campfire in the night
Burning spirit of delight
Teach me how to see the light
Let me learn to warm the heart
Deep within your flame is Father Sun
All things are one
For He is my Father too
Oh take me back
Take me back
With you.

III

Make my bed beneath a cedar tree
Let the night winds speak to me
Tell me of the times that used to be
Tell me of the times to come
Oh thou holy earth
What have we done
We men who live?
Will there be time to forgive?
Oh take me back my friend
Take me back with you
Take me back
Take me back
Again.

Hub Miller 1973

Across this Silent Canvas

George Hubbard Miller

January 24, 1934 — December 25, 1982